D1472119

People

Celebrates

All My Children

A chronicle of
the show's 41 years of
memorable scenes,
crazy characters,
groundbreaking plots
and legendary stars

Contents

94

122

116

41 *Years Ago*
on the outskirts of Philadelphia...

. . . A quirky little town known as Pine Valley was founded. The place was populated with scheming powerbrokers, lust-crazed housewives and oddball characters. Fittingly, the town's debut came with surprisingly little melodrama. "When ABC asked me to create a show, I said, 'Okay, but I want to deal with subjects that are socially relevant and often taboo,'" says *All My Children*'s mastermind, Agnes Nixon, 83, who had previously worked on *Guiding Light* and *Another World* and launched *One Life to Live*. Nixon's concept for *AMC* had already been rejected by Procter and Gamble. But her golden touch for creating must-see daytime fare ultimately convinced ABC to allow the groundbreaking on Pine Valley to begin.

"One of the things that Agnes does so well is to bring in contemporary issues," says one of the show's longtime writers, Lorraine Broderick. "When the Vietnam War was going on, that was on the show, then the beginning of the AIDS epidemic, then a wife-abuse story line, and of course the iconic intervention when Erica's brother Mark was a

Agnes Nixon in a cameo appearance on *AMC* in 2008.

cocaine addict." For Nixon, Pine Valley was a real American town. "Someone once said to me, 'Things don't happen in real life the way they do on soap operas,'" recalls Nixon. "And I said, 'Do you read the daily news headlines? Yes, they do!'"

But all the hot-button stories in the world wouldn't attract an audience if viewers didn't care about the characters. "For Agnes to take the character of Erica Kane and focus a full show on a teenager, not an adult—it was unheard of at the time," says *AMC*'s current executive producer Julie Hanan Carruthers. "It was just explosive."

Even Nixon admits, "She was the first of her kind. I needed to write a character who would say and do the things that I wished I could. Women relate to her because she is speaking for them. And men love her because she's feisty and beautiful." After Erica, Nixon created a lot of unforgettable characters. "Ultimately, I write about sin and redemption," she says. "The characters all have to resonate with the audience. Even the ones who are nuts or evil or having bad times, the audience has to say, 'There but for the grace of God, go I.'"

A map of Pine Valley commissioned by the show's producers in 1995.

The Woman BEHIND ERICA

Susan Lucci

How she went from aspiring actress to being the most famous vixen in daytime-TV history

Fresh out of Marymount College, Susan Lucci thought she could never have a career in television. "I had dark eyes, olive skin and my hair was dark and naturally curly," says Lucci. "I was told that I looked too ethnic." Her hair was showing the full effects of a humid New York summer day when she went on her first go-see in 1969—for the part of a rebellious teenager on an upcoming daytime TV drama. "I tied a scarf around my head before meeting the casting director and the producer," she says. "As I was leaving, they asked me if I had any questions. I said, 'Do you want to see my hair?' " she recalls, laughing. "They said, 'No it's fine.' " Five callbacks later, Lucci was offered her first major role.

Photographs by ANDREW SOUTHAM

1947
A 1-year-old Lucci poses for a portrait with a stuffed animal.

Still, she was apprehensive about committing to a long-term project. "Signing a three-year contract was almost like doing high school or college all over again, and I wasn't sure," says Lucci. "But I knew the part was wonderful, and whoever wrote it was brilliant." At first, creator Agnes Nixon didn't realize what a perfect fit Lucci was for the role. "I wasn't thinking, 'Oh, there's the girl,'" says Nixon. "But something in Susan made me know she could do it. And now she's created Erica just as much as I have."

Born in 1946 in Yonkers, N.Y., Lucci was the first daughter for her parents, Victor, a first-generation Italian American who co-owned a construction firm, and Jeanette, a fashionable homemaker who gave up a career as an OR nurse to raise Lucci and her older brother Jimmy. Lucci recalls a childhood filled with trips to historic places like West Point and Fort Ticonderoga, since her father was a major history buff. And although her *AMC* character would be constantly at odds with her mother, Mona, Lucci's relationship with her own mom was more serene. The two would go on mother-daughter dates, day-tripping to New York City to take in a Broadway matinee and then a meal at Sardi's restaurant. But Lucci also went through a typical teen-rebellion stage. "My mother and I would always laugh at the Erica-and-Mona scenes," says Lucci. "It seemed very realistic to us: 15-year-old girls do roll their eyes at their mothers."

It was during her teens—while attending Garden City High School on Long Island—that Lucci's love for theater was sparked by her first acting teacher. Later, at Marymount, she continued her acting studies—taking classes with professors who'd graduated from the Yale School of Drama.

Soon after college, and just four months before beginning the role of the woman who would become synonymous with the term "man-eater," Lucci married Austrian-born Helmut Huber, whom she met in 1964 when she waited tables at the Garden City Hotel, where he'd been executive chef. They'll celebrate their 42nd anniversary this month. "He is just fantastic," she says.

"He's very self-assured, which is something I've always liked about him. I'm really lucky." Huber is equally smitten. "She's as beautiful inside as she is outside," he says, adding that he's never been fazed by her countless TV romances. "She comes home to me every night!" In 1975 Lucci and Huber had daughter Liza. Son Andreas, now an entrepreneur, came along in 1980. The work schedule on *All My Children* turned out to be a good fit for the young mom. "I didn't want them to miss out on anything, and I didn't want to miss anything," she says. "So I'd make

The Look
OF ERICA KANE: HOW SUSAN LUCCI DOES IT

STAYING TRIM "I eat fish, grilled vegetables and fruit," says Lucci, who also avoids snacking. "But there are times I cheat and have pasta!" As for exercise, the fitness buff loves to play tennis and is a devotee of Pilates.

BEAUTY REGIMEN "Susan has incredible bone structure," says Thecla Luisi, the head of the hair-and-makeup department for *AMC*, who plays up Lucci's eyes. "She usually uses a little concealer, foundation, lip color, blush and eyeliner, but she doesn't like liquid liner. It's too harsh." Her hair routine is low-key, says her stylist Valerie Jackson: "She doesn't use a lot of products. She likes to be natural but sexy. She's very into sexy hair!"

1970

1971   1972   1973

1981   1982   1983

1991   1992   1993

2001   2002   2003

Erica
Through the Years

From a glowing teen to the queen of Pine Valley, here are 41 faces of the memorable Ms. Kane

1974   1975   1976   1977   1978   1979   1980

1984   1985   1986   1987   1988   1989   1990

1994   1995   1996   1997   1998   1999   2000

2004   2005   2006   2007   2008   2009   2010

1964
Lucci in her yearbook photo from Garden City High School on Long Island.

their lunches and take time off when they had school vacations. I wanted to be present in their lives." Now that Liza (who is launching Sage Spoonfuls, a product line for moms) has three children of her own, Lucci uses her downtime to dote on her grandkids. "She's wonderful," gushes Liza, who says her kids call Lucci "Grammy." "They go to my parents' house to swim and have lunch and have pizza parties."

In the mid-1980s, with her family life squared away, and with more than a decade of playing Erica clocked in, Lucci decided to capitalize on her daytime-TV success. "As an actress, I didn't want to play just one part, so I started to do TV movies," she says. She starred in fare like NBC's *Mafia Princess* in 1986 and ABC's 1991 murder mystery *The Woman Who Sinned*. Later she branched out into Broadway, playing the lead role of Annie Oakley in the 1990s musical revival *Annie Get Your Gun*. "She's the hardest-working woman in show business," says Lucci's longtime pal Regis Philbin, who asked her to

join him on the road doing cabaret in 1999. "She had a delightful voice," he says. "It was exciting for people to see her in person—not playing that character but being herself and singing a song. I felt the love of the audience for her."

But being Erica Kane did provide Lucci with one opportunity that no other form of entertainment could match: living out almost every crazy fantasy she could imagine. She played a Vegas showgirl, a nun on the run, her own evil döppelganger and, in one particularly memorable arc, a fashion model. "I got to twirl in front of the fountain at Lincoln Center in little tiny dresses," remembers Lucci, who at 5′2″ does not meet the supermodel height requirement. "And I got to climb up on the pedestal of the Statue of Liberty." Earlier in her run on *AMC,* she also triumphed during a historic stand-off with a grizzly bear. "I didn't know how the bear was going to take my yelling at it, but I think we got it in one take," she says. No matter what scenario the character found herself in, Erica resonated with fans. "She was never meant to be one to

emulate in any way," says Lucci. "But women liked that she was strong-willed and that she followed her dreams."

The same could be said for Lucci. Now that the *AMC* part of her life may be coming to an end, Lucci, who also has a successful line of beauty and fashion products sold through HSN, is looking forward to taking a break, but she has no intention of slowing down. "I'm going to start working with my voice teacher and start singing again, because I miss that part of my life," she says. In fact, she's set to do another cabaret gig with Philbin in Palm Beach this December. Rumors have also been swirling about prime-time TV offers coming her way. "She's so good at comedy," says Huber. "So my wish would be for her to get a sitcom and shoot it in New York." Lucci, meanwhile, has just one main hope for the next phase of her career—"to find parts that excite me as much as the part of Erica Kane," she says. Philbin has no doubt that she'll achieve that goal as well. "Susan understands who she is and what she has to do," he says. "And nothing deters her from accomplishing that."

Susan Lucci
FILLS IN THE BLANKS

When people see me at the grocery store, they always ask me… Do you eat? I say, "Absolutely!" I never want to miss a meal.
Erica would have… Grabbed that Emmy for herself a long time ago.
But I… Never would do that.
If I could take one thing from Erica's closet it would be… Whatever I want. I can and I will. The show is ending, and they're going to sell everything!
The biggest perk of being Erica Kane is… The joy of playing the part.
When I stop playing Erica, I will… Miss her like crazy!

1969
Lucci carried a bouquet of gardenias, her grandmother's favorite flower, when she married Huber in Garden City, N.Y., on Sept. 13.

1999
After 19 nominations Lucci finally won a Daytime Emmy. "I was thrilled," she says. Says her husband with a laugh of the epic night: "The ride home was certainly enjoyable!"

2005
Lucci (with her husband, Helmut, daughter Liza, and son Andreas) received a star on the Hollywood Walk of Fame.

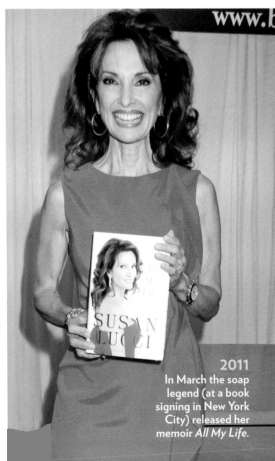

2011
In March the soap legend (at a book signing in New York City) released her memoir *All My Life*.

All My Husbands

The many marriages of Erica Kane-Martin-Brent-Cudahy-Roy-Roy-Chandler-Chandler-Montgomery-Marick-Montgomery

Say what you will about Erica Kane, but having had eight husbands (three of whom she married more than once), it's clear that she's not prone to getting cold feet on her way to the altar. "Erica has a never-ending quest for love," says Lucci, who reunited with all of her fictional spouses on *Oprah* earlier this year. "She believes in marriage, and she doesn't blame the institution of marriage for the lack of love—she wants both and that perfect man for her. Maybe she's just somebody in love with the hunt, I really don't know, but she keeps looking."

1
JEFF MARTIN
(1971)

Erica's marriage to the med student (Charles Frank) may have been doomed from the start; as a young go-getter, she was more set on a modeling career than being a stay-at-home wife. Still, Lucci remembers the onscreen relationship as being "very romantic."

2
PHIL BRENT
(1975)

When Erica became pregnant with his child, Phil Brent (then Nicholas Benedict) persuaded her to marry him. Sadly their joy didn't last. After suffering a miscarriage, Erica had a nervous breakdown and was committed to a mental institution. "They were not well matched," sums up Lucci.

3
TOM CUDAHY
(1978)

"I had one of the highlight experiences of my career in that relationship, because we went to St. Croix for 10 days filming the honeymoon," says Richard Shoberg. "Susan was a huge star even then. I wasn't, but she was so kind and very professional."

4
MIKE ROY
(1984 & 1985)

"It turned out not to be legal, but we thought we were married!" says Lucci of her union with writer Mike Roy (Nicolas Surovy). At first "I was unimpressed with Erica. I was reluctant," recalls Surovy of his character. "But Susan and I got along very well. It was great fun."

5
ADAM
CHANDLER
(1984 & 1991)

Chandler blackmailed Erica to get her to agree to a second marriage. "I figured I must've done something right the first time, so I tried it again," says David Canary of his character's motivation. "It was like *War of the Roses*," Lucci has said of their rocky pairing.

6
TRAVIS
MONTGOMERY
(1988 & 1990)

"They put me on-camera with Susan to get an idea of what the chemistry was," recalls Larkin Malloy. "I'm close to 6 ft. and she's 5'2", but as it turned out, we had the most interesting chemistry."

7
DIMITRI MARICK
(1993 & 1994)

The Hungarian count (ex-*Dynasty* star Michael Nader) had a fiery relationship with Erica—she ended up stabbing him in the chest while having a rape flashback. "I learned a lot from her," says Nader of Lucci. "I saw how she assimilated material quickly and found her moments."

8
JACKSON
MONTGOMERY
(2005)

"We had these misadventures," says Walt Willey. "It was actually the fans who said, 'We like these two together.' All of a sudden, they put us together, and I realized I was working with the top of the pyramid."

"I loved Erica Kane from the moment I read my first audition scene, and I will always love her. She made me feel like I can fly"

—Susan Lucci

"I was five months pregnant," says Lucci when her character Erica (with her brother Mark) opened a disco in 1979. "I remember thinking, 'Oh yeah, this is hidden.' But I remember going on to watch, and I was as big as a house."

The 1970s

"The show always had a mandate to inform as well as entertain. The story lines about drug addiction and gay teens ... it was groundbreaking"

—Susan Lucci

1970

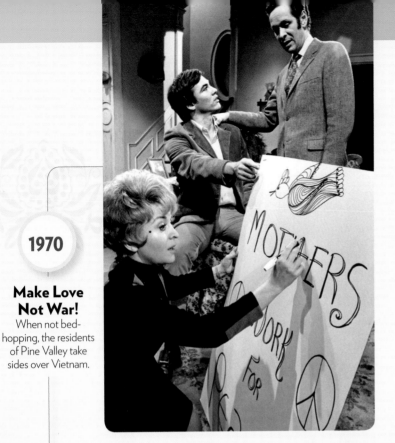

Make Love Not War!
When not bed-hopping, the residents of Pine Valley take sides over Vietnam.

Erica Gets an Abortion
The controversial plot begins mere months after *Roe v. Wade*. (Later it's revealed that the abortion never actually took place; see 2005).

1973

Pine Valley protests the war

1972

Big Wedding!
Setting the stage for four decades of family melodrama, widower Dr. Joe Martin and nurse Ruth Brent tie the knot at the groom's home.

1974

Real-Life Face-Lift
Agnes Nixon works actress Eileen Letchworth's plastic surgery into the show, exploring the psychological effects.

1973

Tad Arrives
An abused, abandoned child turns up at Pine Valley Hospital and goes on to become one of the most beloved characters in *AMC* history.

1975

Murder Victim

After finally finding happiness by marrying Dr. Jeff Martin, nurse Mary Kennicott is shot and killed by burglars.

1977

A Tragic Death

Diagnosed with an inoperable brain tumor, Kitty Shea Tyler insists on living out her last days at home rather than in the hospital. She dies with husband Linc by her side.

1979

Senior Love Triangle

Mona blackmails Phoebe into divorcing Dr. Charles Tyler so that she can have him for herself.

...nd an actress gets a face-lift

1976

Forbidden Love

Donna Beck, a 16-year-old prostitute, lands in the hospital and steals the heart of Dr. Chuck Tyler.

1978

A New Dynasty

The wealthy and conniving Palmer Cortlandt—along with his beloved daughter Nina—moves into town and immediately starts stirring up trouble.

EVIL GENIUS

After Dixie escaped Tuggle's clutches, he did his best to get between her and her life-long love, Tad. Tuggle met his demise when he fell off a bridge while struggling with Tad. "I had such a wonderful, wonderful time playing in that soap opera," says Cowles.

BEAUTY AND THE BEAST

Veteran theater actor and playwright Matthew Cowles—the man who created the character of Billy Clyde Tuggle—has been married to *The Good Wife* star Christine Baranski since 1983. They have two daughters. Still a working actor, Cowles, 66, last appeared in the 2010 thriller *Shutter Island*.

A CAPTIVE AUDIENCE

After running a ring of teenage prostitutes, Tuggle branched out into kidnapping—holding Dixie hostage in a secluded cabin.

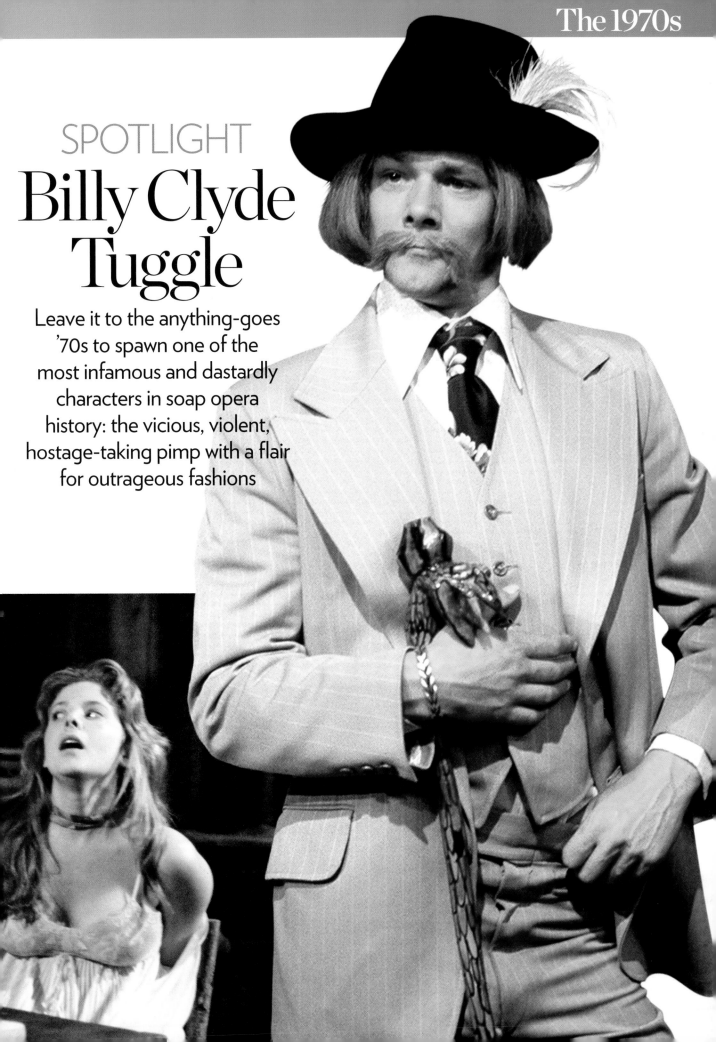

SPOTLIGHT

Billy Clyde Tuggle

Leave it to the anything-goes '70s to spawn one of the most infamous and dastardly characters in soap opera history: the vicious, violent, hostage-taking pimp with a flair for outrageous fashions

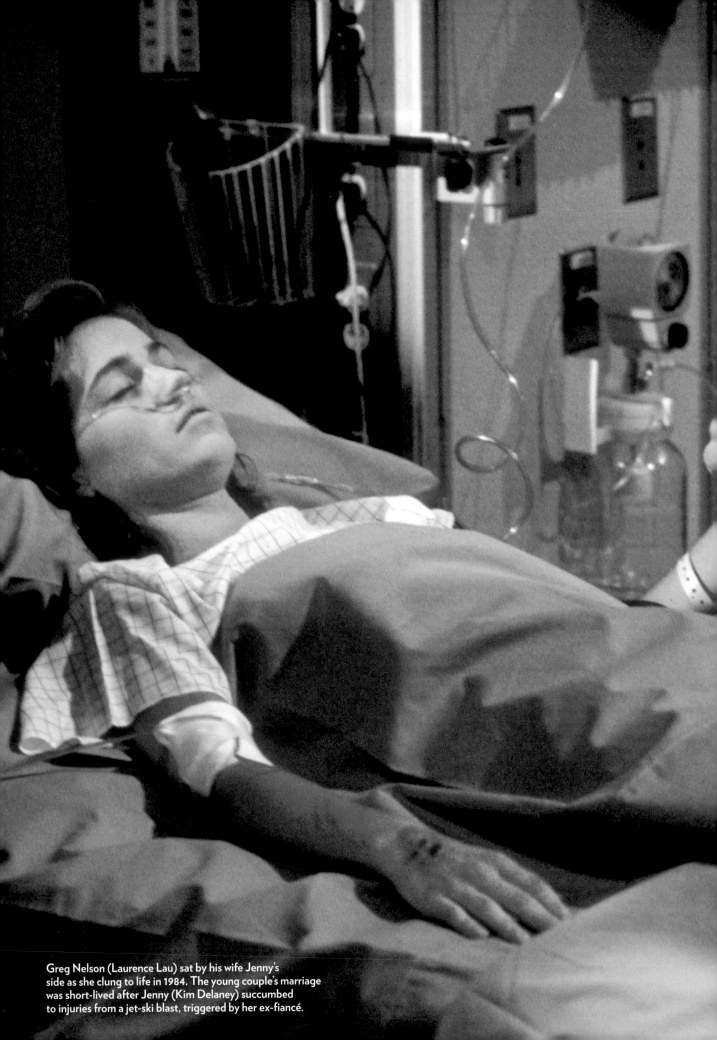

Greg Nelson (Laurence Lau) sat by his wife Jenny's side as she clung to life in 1984. The young couple's marriage was short-lived after Jenny (Kim Delaney) succumbed to injuries from a jet-ski blast, triggered by her ex-fiancé.

The 1980s

"The Greg-and-Jenny story line was a real Romeo and Juliet with high school kids"

—Michael E. Knight

1982

Avalanche!

Divorced couple Chuck and Donna get stranded on a Swiss mountainside. After taking refuge in a cave, the two rekindle their passion, and Donna becomes pregnant.

1980

Star-Crossed Lovers

After years of being manhandled by her pimp, prostitute Estelle finally gets together with Phoebe's chauffeur Benny.

1983

Tad Sleeps with Liza... and Her Mom!

"Tad the Cad" tries to juggle young love and sex with a cougar—with disastrous results.

Tad gets caught in a love triangle and

1983

Erica: The Movie

Obsessed with achieving film stardom, Erica gets involved with the conniving Adam Chandler, who buys the rights to her autobiography *Raising Kane*.

1981

Baby Drama

Sybil—the woman who tries to come between Cliff and Nina—gives birth to Cliff's child but soon gets killed by a hired thug.

1983

Bonkers the Cat

The feline received some 45 fan letters a month—more than owner Daisy Cortlandt.

1986

Prison Break
Attempting to bust Jeremy out of jail, Erica stages a faux wedding and a daring helicopter escape—to no avail.

Jesse Dies . . . Sort of
A fatal gunshot to the abdomen claims the life of one of Pine Valley's finest. Nevertheless Jesse returns in 2008.

Pine Valley Bulletin

COP DIES A HERO

Detective Jesse Hubba

EXCLUSIVE ... TS ON PAGE 2

1988

Erica learns her father's secret

1989

Erica's Dad Is a Clown
A trip to the circus reveals that the man who abandoned Erica all those years ago is now known as Barney the Clown.

1985

Bear Attack!
The year of the infamous *AMC* scene in which Erica comes face-to-face with a grizzly. "You may not come near me!" she yells. "I am Erica Kane and you are a filthy beast!"

1987

Intervention!
When her brother Mark Dalton gets beaten up while trying to score some drugs, Erica orchestrates a family intervention. He finally agrees to enter rehab.

1988

Birth of Bianca
Despite a bout with toxemia, Erica gives birth to a healthy baby girl— Bianca Christine Montgomery.

Glamorama

The place to go to get your hair and makeup done—and to get a fix of the owner's folksy charm

TRESS FOR SUCCESS

When Opal opened the Glamorama in 1982, it became a go-to hangout for the women of Pine Valley (including Opal's daughter Jenny, below). In fact, when the salon was later robbed, there was a whopping $1,500 in the cash register.

RINSE & REPEAT

Tad used his job as a shampoo boy to hit on women.

OPENING DAY
The beauty shop drew a big crowd.

READY FOR BUSINESS
Opal (first played by Dorothy Lyman) got the money to open up her salon by blackmailing the married man she was having an affair with—Langley Wallingford.

THE 1980s
Super Couples

STUART & CINDY

After Agnes Nixon and the network decided to do a story about AIDS, head writer Lorraine Broderick wanted to be sure that viewers were deeply invested in Cindy (Ellen Wheeler), who had the disease. "I thought if we're going to play this emotional, heart-wrenching story, it would be so much more powerful if it was a love story," she recalls. "I came up with the idea of Stuart [David Canary] falling in love with her. It was his first love story." Her plan worked: "When she finally died, everyone cared about Cindy."

GREG & JENNY

"They had a sweet innocence that was really wonderful to watch," says Broderick of the teenage lovebirds, played by Laurence Lau and Kim Delaney. "But they had huge obstacles to overcome: Greg's mother was a snob, and Jenny was from the wrong side of the tracks." And despite her character's tragic death by jet-ski, Delaney has nothing but good memories from her time on the soap. "We had so many good times," she says. "It was an incredible first job."

NINA & CLIFF

"When we were Cliff and Nina, we had this magic that happened," Taylor Miller says of her chemistry with onscreen beau Peter Bergman. "It was a little bit of that Cinderella thing. He was able to get me down from the ivory tower, and I think that's what every girl dreams of." Their romance had such an impact that three decades later, fans still approach him, says Bergman. "They say, 'I love Cliff and Nina!'"

ANGIE & JESSE

In 1981, despite her father's wishes, well-to-do Angie (Debbi Morgan) fell for former busboy Jesse (Darnell Williams) and ignited one of *AMC*'s most heartwarming couples. Morgan recalls trying to see a movie with Williams near Times Square when they were spotted—and chased—by ardent viewers. "You would've thought we were Michael and Janet Jackson," she says of the chaos. "It was mind-boggling." Their partnership induced so much fan appreciation that even though Jesse "died" in 1988 (it was later revealed he faked his death), viewers never gave up on the couple. "We had focus groups, and they'd always say, 'We miss Jesse and Angie,'" says creator Agnes Nixon. "So I said, 'Well, let's bring them back.' [They did in 2008.] Somebody would say, 'But he's dead,' and I would say, 'Well, so what? It was such a beautiful love story.'"

Morgan and Williams in June 2011

Erica finally gets the chance to confront the man who attacked her on her 14th birthday.

The
1990s

"Erica was strong. She had
an ability to express herself
and not be victimized, even though
she had been raped"

—Susan Lucci

1990

Billy Clyde Tuggle Is Back!

After prison, the pimp returns. He kidnaps Dixie and tries to kill Tad, before dying in a fall from a bridge.

Evil Twin

In a dual role for actress Kate Collins, "Janet from Another Planet" pushes sis Natalie into a well and then usurps her life, including her romance with Trevor.

Kelly Ripa meets her match and

1992

1991

A Perilous Fire

After a bomb goes off, Trevor rushes to the rescue of his wife, Natalie. She survives the blast but ends up losing her vision.

Erica's Surprise Daughter

Kendall Hart (Sarah Michelle Gellar) goes to work for Erica and soon discovers she's her boss's daughter. Kendall's father is Richard Fields, the man who raped Erica in the '70s.

1994

O.J. vs. AMC

The national obsession with the O.J. Simpson murder case leads ABC to preempt the soap .

1993

The Chicken Shack Arc

When high-and-mighty Palmer Cortlandt goes bankrupt, he's forced to don an apron and a paper hat and work at the lowly fast-food restaurant.

1995

Kelly Ripa Meets Future Husband

Marc Consuelos joins the cast as Mateo Santos. He ends up marrying Ripa's character.

1996

A Trip to Betty Ford

Erica becomes addicted to painkillers and mimics stars like Liza Minnelli and Elizabeth Taylor by checking into rehab.

AMC takes time out for O.J.

1997

Bianca Gets Anorexia

Erica's teenage daughter begins to waste away from an eating disorder. Her mom convinces her to get help.

1998

Hero Dog

Harold the pooch saves the day by sniffing out the truth about crazy Janet posing as her sister Natalie.

1999

Car Crash Nearly Kills Erica

Erica and David Hayward get into a serious wreck, which leaves Erica's face disfigured. The plot mirrors a real-life accident that Lucci had in 1966, which left her with a permanent facial scar.

GOING
GOTH

A GRAPE
DISASTER

EXTREME
RINGLETS

Hayley's Hair Don'ts

Kelly Ripa's character showcased a horror show of styles—from badly dyed to curiously curly

SWOOPING
IT UP

BANGS
GONE BAD

SPLIT
ENDS

HAYLEY AND MATEO

Though Adam Chandler's daughter Hayley (Kelly Ripa) had a dramatic and often-rocky relationship with Mateo Santos (Mark Consuelos), offscreen the two had a much easier go of things, tying the knot in Vegas in 1996 after just a few months of dating. They now have three children, Michael, 14, Lola, 10, and Joaquin, 8. "It was a big part of our lives," Ripa has said about *All My Children.* "[We] met there, and we had our [first two] children there."

Super Couples

DIXIE AND TAD

"I remember the first scene we did together: Dixie was pregnant by Adam, and I was the kid from the wrong side of the tracks," recalls Michael E. Knight (Tad) of working with Cady McClain (Dixie). "They weren't supposed to be together, but it had a life of its own." For the next two decades, they shared a passionate romance on the show and still have a friendship. Says McClain: "I adore him."

EDMUND AND MARIA

As the new surgeon in town, Maria (Eva LaRue) quickly fell for news reporter Edmund (John Callahan) and married him. (The two were also wed in real life from 1996 to 2004.) "We were falling in love offscreen, and it was so romantic," LaRue recalls of the TV wedding. And then came parenthood: Maria and Edmund went on to have two kids, while the stars who played them had a daughter in 2001.

JULIA AND NOAH

Her onscreen family wasn't pleased about Julia (Sydney Penny) being in an interracial relationship with Noah (Keith Hamilton Cobb), but the two were a charismatic duo. "I don't know that they intended the couple to be long-term, but it just worked," says Penny. "They tried pairing me with other characters and nothing clicked. I think that's why this was so successful—it was completely organic."

Soon after arriving in Pine Valley, Greenlee finds herself in danger.

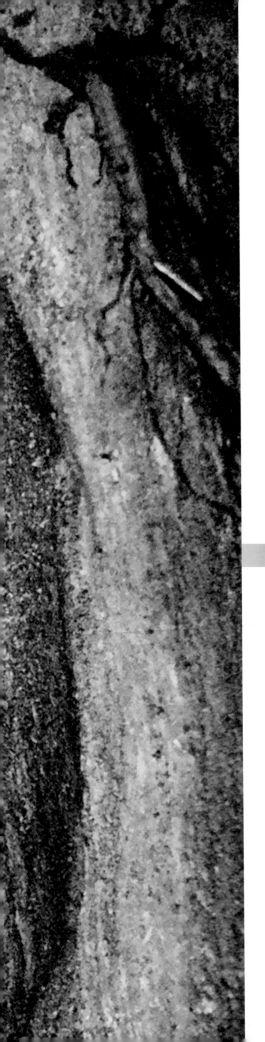

The
2000s

"Some characters just pop—
sometimes they're more fun or
naughtier or have an agenda.
When I cast Rebecca Budig as
Greenlee, it was so terrific"

—*AMC* **casting director Judy Blye Wilson**

Hostage Drama

Greenlee—who has been terrorized by Pine Valley drug lord Vanessa Bennett (aka Proteus)—barely survives being kidnapped by the menace.

2000

Bianca Comes Out

Erica struggles to accept that her daughter is gay. "Maybe you just haven't found the right man," she says. But soon Erica gives Bianca her full support.

Terror, mystery, disasters and

2001

Amnesia!

The character Anna Devane, who was wildly popular on *General Hospital*, pops up in Pine Valley with memory loss.

2003

Fake Pregnancy

While she is on trial for the murder of Michael Cambias, Kendall's expectant-mom ploy is exposed as a fraud when Greenlee yanks off Kendall's top to reveal there's only padding where the baby bump should be.

2005

Fertility Freak-Out
Dr. Greg Madden (above left) is the man who performed Erica's abortion. Turns out he's a fertility expert and actually implanted Erica's fetus into his wife who gave birth to a son, Josh (who happens to be Erica's new assistant).

2006

Gender Bender
In a story line that garners national media attention, AMC introduces a transgender character: Zarf (Jeffrey Carlson) is transitioning from a man to a woman (Zoe).

2004

Baby Switch
After months of believing that her daughter Miranda was killed in a crash shortly after being born, Bianca discovers that she's alive—Babe Chandler had swapped her for her dead son.

gay rights define the decade

2008

Tornado!
When a natural disaster strikes, Pine Valley is thrown into chaos. Houses are in rubble, people are missing and the storm claims one major casualty—Babe Chandler.

2007

Ryan Rescues Kendall
Right before the Satin Slayer (Alexander Cambias) was poised to claim his final victim, Ryan saves the day.

2009

Who Killed Stuart?
Mistaken for being his scheming twin brother, Adam, Stuart gets shot and killed. There are a number of suspects, but the murderer turns out to be . . . Kendall.

SPOTLIGHT

AMC Does Reality TV

Keeping up with the times, the stars of Pine Valley waltzed their way onto TV's talent competitions. One even skated off with the top prize

A LEG UP
Aiden Turner got to rumba with legendary *Dancing with the Stars* pro Edyta Sliwinska during the show's spring 2010 season. He came in ninth.

CHAMP!
Rebecca Budig beat Bethenny Frankel for top honors on 2010's *Skating with the Stars*.

POWER PAIR
Like Turner, Cameron
Mathison partnered
with Sliwinska during
his 2007 *Dancing* stint.
He placed fifth.

MAKING HER MOVE
In the fall 2008 season of *Dancing with
the Stars*, Lucci paired up with pro Tony
Dovolani (who later made a cameo on *All
My Children*) and ended up in sixth place.

THE 2000s
Super Couples

BABE & JR

"My favorite story line was with Babe [Alexa Havens]," says Jacob Young, who has played JR Chandler since 2003. The tale of two ill-fated lovers was so hot, says Young, it even persuaded a TV channel in France to pick up the series. "Babe dying in my arms was one of the hardest scenes to play," he adds of the couple's tragic end. "But we worked it."

AMANDA & JAKE

Despite the lies, the flings and the STD, Dr. Martin and his wife clocked a lot of hours in bed. "My mom's like, 'Gosh, it's disgusting, all the kissing—don't doctors have more important things to do?'" says Ricky Paull Goldin. Meanwhile, the other half of the popular duo is just trying to deal with Amanda's sexual shame. "I used to joke that the only thing I wouldn't do as an actor is a herpes commercial," says Chrishell Stause. "Cut to six years later, and I'm basically doing a herpes PSA. Go get checked out, kids—keep your knees together!"

KENDALL & ZACH

"Kendall and Zach were always going through drama," says Alicia Minshew of her onscreen husband (played by her close friend Thorsten Kaye). "There were sad stories, like almost losing our son, and fun ones, like when we got to go to Vegas dressed as members of the Mafia, that always gave us something powerful to play. Whenever I work with him, it's electric."

RYAN & GREENLEE

"Ryan and Greenlee have gone through so many crazy ups and downs that it's kind of tough to believe that this is going to work," admits Cameron Mathison. "But we have an unparalleled connection." Adds Rebecca Budig: "They have a deep, different kind of love—a rare and lasting one." In real life, Mathison and Budig have a similar (though completely platonic!) bond: "I'm Scooby-doo," says Mathison. "And I'm Scrappy!" chirps Budig. "I swear to God, I come into work and I'm so happy to see his face."

My Favorite Memories

The current cast talks about the moments they'll remember, what they'll miss most and their post-Pine Valley plans

VINCENT IRIZARRY

"DR. EVIL" DAVID HAYWARD

"I've had more staged fights on this show than I'll ever have in my life," says Irizarry, 51. "I've been flipped over people's backs, over couches; I'm convinced that 'Dr. Dave' has a titanium jaw and face, because nothing ever injures him."

JACOB YOUNG
SCHEMING JR CHANDLER

"I'm finishing my first film script and I've got a couple TV pilots that I've written," says Young, 31, of his post-*AMC* plans. "I also produce a little one-woman show with Joan Collins, so we're flying out to Australia to do that."

KATE COLLINS
PSYCHO KILLER JANET DILLON

"What I love about my character is that she has no self-edit at all," says Collins, 52. "She's the freest, most fun, I've ever been able to be. There's almost nothing you can't say or do."

CADY McCLAIN
DEATH-DEFYING DIXIE MARTIN

"The phone call asking me to come back was a beautiful way to say, 'Okay, look, crazy things happen on soaps; mistakes are made,'" says McClain, 41. "They said, 'Let's see if we can make this right and put this back on track while we still have the time to do it.'"

ALICIA MINSHEW
DAMSEL IN DISTRESS KENDALL HART SLATER

"When the show ends, I want to steal some of my purses, dresses and jewelry!" says Minshew, 37. "And Kendall's piano— if they would put strings in it!"

DARNELL WILLIAMS
HERO COP JESSE HUBBARD

"I'm a pretty good interior designer," says Williams, 56. "It's something I would love to explore after *All My Children*."

RICKY PAULL GOLDIN
LADIES' MAN JAKE MARTIN

"People scream across a crowded airport, 'Don't break Amanda's heart!'" says Goldin, 46, of running into *AMC* fans. "It's gotten a little bit crazy."

All My Children
IS MY
HOME

Michael E. Knight

The actor who has played quirky P.I. Tad Martin for 30 years reflects on what made him return to the show after leaving twice

When Michael E. Knight nabbed the role of Tad Martin straight out of acting school at age 22, he wasn't convinced he could pull off the "cocksure, arrogant ladies' man" persona producers wanted. "I was a wallflower in college—women were a total mystery to me," says Knight, now 52, whose first major story line involved romancing teenager Liza Colby *and* her mom, Marian. "So I asked, 'Does he have to be so despicable? Can he be funny?'" That sense of humor became Tad's calling card, and, Knight believes, it's the reason his character has maintained a loyal fan base through bouts of amnesia, a murder charge, multiple affairs and fickle network executives "who wondered whether the character had reached his expiration date."

Now, almost 30 years and three Daytime Emmys later, Knight—who's divorced after a 14-year marriage to former *One Life to Live* star Catherine Hickland—realizes how lucky he has been. "As a young man, I thought this was a stepping stone—like, 'Wait till I get my nighttime series,'" says Knight, who left *AMC* twice to pursue film and prime-time TV roles (he starred in the 1987 movie *Date with an Angel* and episodes of *Murder, She Wrote* and *Matlock*). But when other leading-man roles didn't arise, he returned to Pine Valley. "*All My Children* was my home to go back to," he says. "A steady paycheck and a place where you were appreciated. I remember one of the last moments of *Cheers* when Ted Danson looks at the bar and says, 'I'm the luckiest son of a bitch on earth.' That's how I feel."

REBECCA BUDIG
VIXEN
GREENLEE SMYTHE

"I don't have a ton of crazy fan stories," says Budig, 37, "but this one woman recognized me and shouted, 'Greenlee! Greenlee!' She hugged me, then looked me up and down and said, 'You're chunky on TV!' And I was like, 'What? Wow, I guess I'm the fat girl on *All My Children.*'"

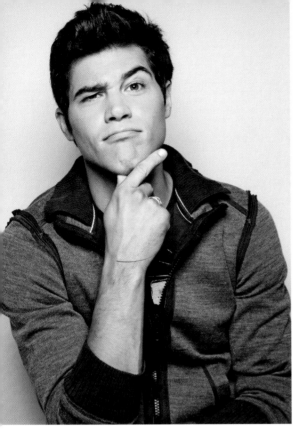

TRENT GARRETT
DREAMBOAT ASHER PIKE

"I do whatever I can to get a laugh," says the former model, 27, of his backstage demeanor. "I'd just go up behind people and put fake snow over them as they were filming."

DEBBI MORGAN
THE SURVIVOR, DR. ANGIE HUBBARD

"It's been really hard not being able to see for so long," says Emmy winner Morgan, 54, who's had to play blind for a year. "There's so much expression that comes through the eyes, so it's been really challenging to try to convey emotion to the audience."

NATALIE HALL
LOVELORN COLBY CHANDLER

"My mother is a huge fan of *All My Children* because of Erica Kane," says Hall, 23. "When I got the part of Colby, my mom asked, 'Who are you related to?' I said, 'Liza Colby.' My mom said, 'I hate Liza Colby!' I said, 'Well, you can't hate her anymore! I'm her daughter.'"

Proud to be a SOAP STAR

Walt Willey

The actor who has played the valiant Jackson Montgomery since 1987 talks about the joys of getting a steady paycheck on a daytime drama

He has spent most of his career in Pine Valley, and Walt Willey, 60, doesn't regret any of it. "I come from a working-class background," says the Ottawa, Ill., native. "To me this has always been a blue-collar job in terms of acting. We are laborers!" Although Willey has never had any official training and didn't even begin to act until he was 30 years old, he did have one major plus going for him. "I worked as an extra on *All My Children* 50 times," he says. "I put Greg in the back of an ambulance; I was Palmer's jet pilot and limo driver. So when it was my time, I was ready to go." Now that Willey will get a break from memorizing 40 pages of script each day, the married father of two looks forward to spending time with his family at their New Mexico ranch, getting more tattoos ("In the next four years, I'll be covered!") and, of course, staying in showbiz. "If I could never create again," he says, "that would be the end of my world."

JENNIFER BASSEY
**RESIDENT COUGAR
MARIAN COLBY CHANDLER**

"When Mikey [Michael E. Knight] and I did love scenes, I asked him where he was going to put his feet, " recalls Bassey, 72. "He said, 'Why?' I said, 'We can't be awkward. We have to rehearse. I'm going to play with your chest hair here. Then I'm going to reach for my purse over your body here and climb on top of you.' We'd laugh till we were sick, but it worked!"

JORDI VILASUSO
DO-GOODER DR. GRIFFIN CASTILLO

"I was really excited to be playing a doctor as opposed to, like, a gangster," says Vilasuso, 30. "I've played a lot of shady characters in movies before, so it was nice that this guy was more of a professional."

J.R. MARTINEZ
TRUE-BLUE COP BROT MONROE

"We joke that my character could have the worst first name in TV history," says Martinez, 28, a real-life Iraq War vet who suffered severe burns when his Humvee hit a land mine. "I tell people that the name is almost the same as what I had to do when I was injured—I had to accept it and make it work."

CAMERON MATHISON
MR. NICE GUY RYAN LAVERY

"When I first got on the show, my character was accused of rape," recalls Mathison, 42. "A fan spotted me in a department store and goes, 'Ryyyyyan! I knew you didn't rape her!' I was the only one who knew she was talking about a story line on TV."

SARAH GLENDENING
SEXUALLY EVOLVING MARISSA TASKER

"My character is easy for me to play because she's assertive," says Glendening, 29, whose onscreen love life took a same-sex twist. "She knows who she is—well, not always [*Laughs*]."

MELISSA CLAIRE EGAN
**CRIMINALLY INSANE
ANNIE LAVERY**

"I remember getting scripts for the scenes where I choke and stab Erica Kane," says Claire, 29. "I thought, 'How am I going to pull this off?' And then Susan Lucci said, 'I don't think I've ever been choked on this show before,' and I thought, 'Oh, my gosh! I did a first with Erica Kane! I choked her!'"

I'm the 7th BIANCA

1	2	3	4	5	6
Jessica Leigh Falborn (1988–1991)	Caroline Wilde (1991)	Lacey Chabert (1992–1993)	Gina Gallagher (1993–1997)	Nathalie Paulding (1997–1998)	Eden Riegel (2000–2010)

Christina Bennett Lind

The actress opens up about the challenges of following six other actresses and how she made the high-profile role her own

Christina Bennett Lind had just six days to prepare to take over the role of Bianca Montgomery. "I found out I got it on a Tuesday, flew to L.A. on Friday and started shooting on Monday," says the native New Yorker, 28. "It was probably a good thing, because I didn't get to think about how terrifying it was!" The scariest part: what the show's fans would think. After all, the sixth Bianca, the beloved Eden Riegel, had embodied the role for nearly a decade. "People thought we looked like each other—that was in my favor," says Lind. It also helped that her predecessor approved. "She gave her blessing right away," says Lind. "Eden sent flowers to the studio after my first week of shooting." When they finally met nearly a year later, "it was weird," laughs Lind. "Like meeting a relative!" Determined to put her own stamp on Bianca, Lind watched only key moments from Bianca's past—her coming out, wedding and rape scenes—"to inform and implant those memories," says Lind. "I realized early on I didn't really have a chance if I wanted to try to mimic Eden." Now, says Lind, she's fallen in love with the role: "This character is such an icon. I feel the responsibility of it, and I'm honored to be a part of that legacy."

JILL LARSON
QUIRKY OPAL CORTLANDT

"I've integrated into the character a lot of Opal-isms that come from my own family," says the two-time Daytime Emmy nominee, 63. "Just the other day, I was looking for the opportunity to use an expression my mother had used, which was, 'Look at what's she's got on! I wouldn't wear that to a dog fight if I knew both dogs!'"

MICHAEL NOURI
POWER BARON CALEB CORTLANDT

"The greatest challenge in this medium is getting the dialogue to make sense," says veteran actor Nouri, 65. "The writers have to come up with so much dialogue for so many characters that sometimes you'll look at a scene and say, 'Who talks like this?'"

STEPHANIE GATSCHET
THE HEARTBROKEN MADISON NORTH

"Madison started as a crazy, manipulative, troubled woman," says Gatschet, 28. " It's been fun to bring the character on a journey. People tell me that they used to hate her, but now they love her."

JAMIE LUNER
SEDUCTRESS LIZA COLBY

"I think I had the most fun during my love affair with Tad," says Luner, 40, of her two years on *AMC*. "We had a really fun, sexy love affair, and Michael Knight is really great to act with. I adore him."

LINDSAY HARTLEY
SPUNKY DR. CARA CASTILLO MARTIN

"I don't have that dream—'Oh, I wish I were a movie star'—I just love to act," says Hartley, 33. "I like playing different people. I'm a very relaxed, chill chick in real life, and I liked that my character was feisty and sarcastic."

CORNELIUS SMITH JR.
STRAIGHT SHOOTER DR. FRANKIE HUBBARD

"I didn't register the magnitude of the role I was getting," says the Daytime Emmy nominee, 29, who's been on since 2007. "It was like, 'You guys want me to play Angie and Jesse's son? Really? Okay . . . now who's Angie and who's Jesse?' My mom had to fill me in."

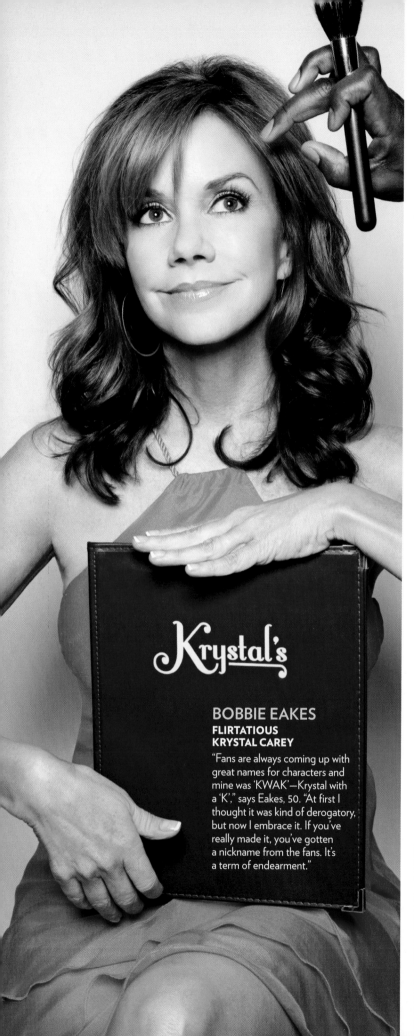

BOBBIE EAKES
FLIRTATIOUS KRYSTAL CAREY

"Fans are always coming up with great names for characters and mine was 'KWAK'—Krystal with a 'K'," says Eakes, 50. "At first I thought it was kind of derogatory, but now I embrace it. If you've really made it, you've gotten a nickname from the fans. It's a term of endearment."

CHRISHELL STAUSE
THE MANIPULATIVE AMANDA DILLON

"This was my first professional TV gig," says Kentucky-born Stause, 30, a former theater actress. When she joined the cast six years ago, Stause recalls being "scared, intimidated and excited, all rolled into one," but now she's grown used to life on a daytime drama. Well, mostly: "The writers don't always tell you what's happening with your character, so I read my script and that's how I found out that I got an STD. I was like, 'Really?! We're about to be off the air and that's how I have to go out?'" Still, Stause knows she's got at least one AMC addict who's always rooting for her. "My grandma is the biggest fan," she says. "She has a huge cardboard cutout with me on it in her home. It's hilarious."

Where ARE THEY NOW?

Artists, teachers, ministers, parents, happy retirees. For these stars, life after *All My Children* has taken surprising—and satisfying—twists and turns

MARCY WALKER
LIZA COLBY

Walker's personal life has been as complex as a soap opera. A veteran of three daytime shows, she has been married five times. Now 49, she goes by the name Marcy Smith (her current husband's surname) and is based in Huntersville, N.C., where she works in Christian ministry.

DAVID CANARY
ADAM AND STUART CHANDLER

The now-retired Canary won five Emmys playing the roles of polar-opposite twins—ruthless Adam and genteel Stuart. "It was hard work," says Canary, 73. "I loved both of them very much. If there were long periods when Stuart wasn't around, I missed him desperately."

MICHAEL B. JORDAN
REGGIE MONTGOMERY

"*All My Children* is where I got my chops," says Jordan, 39, who will next be seen in *Red Tails*. "It opened up a lot of doors for me, and I appreciate the fans that have stayed with me since back then!"

ESTA TERBLANCHE
GILLIAN ANDRASSY

"I was the clumsiest, most ungraceful person ever, and for some reason they always had me in lingerie or naked," says TerBlanche, 38, who now runs her own spa in Valley Village, Calif.

MATT BORLENGHI
BRIAN BODINE

"I will always regret leaving the show after only two years," says Bodine, 44, who now produces reality shows like the upcoming *Jersey Shore*-esque *Persian Princesses*. "I was tired of saying, 'I love you, Hayley' to Kelly Ripa 15 times an episode."

LARKIN MALLOY
TRAVIS MONTGOMERY

An actors' coach with a studio in midtown Manhattan, Malloy, 56, charges $75 per session to help actors audition for roles or generally improve their craft. He also recently starred in a film called *Long Shot Louie* and is an associate producer of a new reality drama. Though he appeared on four soaps, he says, "by far I am most recognized for playing Travis."

FRANCESCA JAMES
KITTY AND HER TWIN, KELLY

Joining the cast in 1972, James, now 62 and living in New York City, was the show's Renaissance woman. Not only did she play two roles, she sang songs that she composed— and then executive produced and directed episodes as late as 2008. "I have a very unusual relationship with *All My Children*," says James, who still directs plays. "I was allowed to wear so many different hats."

EDEN RIEGEL
BIANCA MONTGOMERY

As the sixth Bianca, Riegel, now 30 and an actress on *The Young and the Restless,* got a dream story line: She came out as a lesbian in an emotional arc that won her an Emmy. But her time on *AMC* got her more than an award: "Cameron Mathison introduced me to my husband, Andrew Miller," says Riegel, mother of 5-month-old Jack. And she got something else too: "When you leave, you keep your shoes. I had Jimmy Choos. All my nice shoes are from *All My Children*."

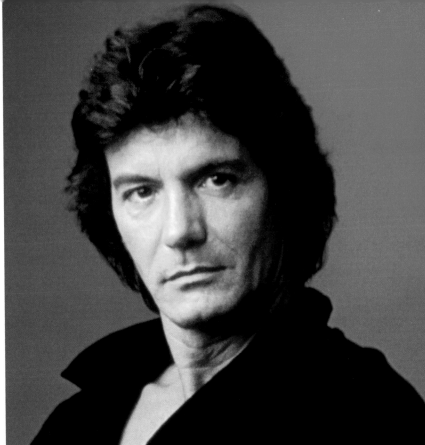

JEAN LECLERC
JEREMY HUNTER

The Quebec-born actor, 63, appears in regional theaters across America and has begun directing plays in Canada, where he lives outside Montreal in an old flour mill built in 1820. "Thanks to *All My Children*, I restored it," says LeClerc. "And last year the government recognized it as a historical monument."

MICHAEL NADER
DIMITRI MARICK

Nader fondly recalls the tortured sibling relationship he had with onscreen brother Edmund. "The years of torment that we caused each other were quite fun." However, he admits it was a sad parting. " I got into some trouble and they let me go." But, says Nader, 66, who lives in California near Lake Tahoe and continues to audition,"I had a ball doing it for 10 years."

SHARI HEADLEY
MIMI REED FRYE

Now 48, she lives in California and is set to begin filming a movie by her pal, actress Troy Byer-Bailey. Meanwhile Headley spends a lot of time with her 17-year-old son, as well as her 85-year-old mother. "I take care of my mother, and I moved her here from New York," says Headley. Another new passion: Twitter, where, she says, "I get so much love from *AMC* fans."

WILLIAM CHRISTIAN
DEREK FRYE

"I could not be happier," says the stay-at-home dad, 55, who lives in Pasadena with his wife, Gail Samuel, and their two sons, Sam, 6, and Orlando, 4. "I have an amazing life. After 15 years on the show, everything I have today on some level is because of *All My Children*."

KAREN LYNN GORNEY
TARA MARTIN

After leaving the show in 1977, she costarred with John Travolta in *Saturday Night Fever*. Now 66, she lives in New York City, where she still acts. She also sells her original paintings on her website karenlynngorney.com.

LINDA GIBBONEY
SYBIL THORNE

She enjoyed playing a villain "because you get to do things you'd never do in real life," says Gibboney, 61, who teaches an after-school arts program in L.A. "I'm teaching the kids self-esteem," she says. "They're little sponges."

SYDNEY PENNY
JULIA SANTOS KEEFER

After a hiatus she is venturing back into TV "in mom roles," says Penny, 39. "What keeps me running now is my son Chasen, who's 4." She's also been traveling and restoring houses with her businessman husband, Robert Powers.

TAYLOR MILLER
NINA CORTLANDT

If you hear a familiar female voice on, say, a State Farm or Quaker Oatmeal commercial, chances are it belongs to Taylor Miller, now 57. After exiting *AMC* in 1989, she moved to Chicago with her husband, Eli Tullis, and, she says, "I've anonymously been doing voice-overs for the past 20 years!" Miller gave up her daytime career to raise Liza, now 22, and Eli, 20. "I couldn't handle being famous and raising children," she says. "So I disappeared." But she did find time to return to *AMC* for cameos over the years. "Nina has really impacted my life," she insists. "People still come up to me and think they know me. How lovely to be a part of something that fabulous!"

JUSTIN BRUENING
JAMIE MARTIN

After their characters married on the show, Bruening proposed to Alexa Havins (who played Babe Chandler) on-set, "and she started crying her eyes out," he recalls. Wed since 2005, Bruening, 32, has appeared in sitcoms and is now "trying to seek out different roles—like villains," he says.

ALEXA HAVINS
BABE CHANDLER

Her job led to something bigger and better: "I met the love of my life," she says of castmate Justin Bruening. "We have a beautiful daughter [Lexington, 1]." Now starring in TV's *Torchwood: Miracle Day*, Havins, 31, says, "I look at *All My Children* now, and we are going to have All Our Children together because of it."

THORSTEN KAYE
ZACH SLATER

Wed to *One Life to Live*'s Susan Haskell and father to McKenna, 8, and Marlowe, 4, Kaye, 45, is a published poet and a sports blogger, as well as an actor. Of *AMC* he says, "In a perfect world, I'd like to work with some of these guys again."

GIL ROGERS
RAY GARDNER

Now 77 and retired, Rogers says, "I'm from Kentucky and used Kentucky-isms. The censor would ask what it means. I'd never say it was one of the dirtiest things on TV."

LAMMAN RUCKER
GARRET WILLIAMS

Rucker, 39, has appeared in Tyler Perry films, Off-Broadway theater productions and, with a business partner, launched a line of sensual body products called Forplai. "I loved *All My Children*," he says. "We had a lot of fun. I loved the culture. Everybody was just supercool."

JOHN CALLAHAN
EDMUND GREY

Callahan, 56, who's still acting in films and TV, not only kept a baseball jacket from his time on the show, he also came away with a wife. The actor married Eva La Rue, who played Edmund's love Maria (the two have since divorced). Says Callahan: "I met the girl I married in real life and also got the best gift any man could ever get—a daughter. That supersedes any lamp, pen or picture frame you could possibly swipe."

DOROTHY LYMAN

OPAL GARDNER

"It's the role that made me famous," says Lyman, who won two Emmy awards as the flamboyant Gardner. The now 64-year-old filmmaker lives on a farm in upstate New York and teaches directing at the New School for Drama in New York City.

JULIA BARR
BROOKE ENGLISH

After surviving numerous legendary cat fights with frenemy Erica Kane, Barr—who won Emmys in 1990 and 1998—has moved into developing web dramedies with her *AMC* costar Jill Larson. But Brooke did make it back to Pine Valley one last time for a scene with her TV husband Adam Chandler. "They gave her a happy ending," says Barr, 62. "She'd never kept a man. It was wonderful closure for both of our characters."

MARK LAMURA
MARK DALTON

He has come a long way from playing Erica's troubled brother. Married with a 12-year-old daughter and living in New York City, he recently appeared in a Disney film and in *Something Borrowed*. "I did four films last year," says LaMura, 61. "I've become Internet savvy. I've gotten films by auditioning on Skype!"

KATHLEEN NOONE
ELLEN DALTON

She still acts—she appeared on *Dexter* last year—but Noone, 66, who lives in L.A., is shifting course. "I've been finishing up becoming a licensed lay minister," she says. "I'd like to work with kids in their 20s who don't know who they are yet." She also enjoys traveling. "I have a rich, full life," she says.

JAMES KIBERD
TREVOR DILLON

While Kiberd, 62, continues to act and direct in New York City, he is also an award-winning painter, and now, he says, "I've started building gardens." He's married to Susan Keith from *Loving*.

TONYA PINKINS
LIVIA FRYE

The theater vet, 49, is in a new play in California called *Milk Like Sugar*. "Being on *AMC* allowed me to do theater, because theater is low-paying," she says.

NICOLAS SUROVY
MIKE ROY

Surovy, 67, is now an artist in California experimenting with painting and sculptures. "I haven't been able to tear myself away from this life that I'm living now," he says.

RICHARD SHOBERG
TOM CUDAHY
After more than 20 years in the role, Shoberg is not surprised that "many more people know me as Tom than as Dick." The actor, 61, can now be seen in the Off-Broadway play *Perfect Crime*.

DONDRE WHITFIELD
TERRENCE FRYE
The Cosby Show vet, 42, is now doing standup comedy in California. But his ties to *AMC* remain strong: He's godfather to the son of Richard Lawson, who played his dad. "We became instant friends," says Whitfield. "It was like we'd known each other our whole lives."

RUDOLF MARTIN
ANTON LANG
AMC producers liked him so much, they created a role for the actor, now 44, who recently finished an indie film and shot a piece with Britney Spears for her concert tour.

BRITTANY ALLEN
MARISSA CHANDLER
Still reeling from her June Daytime Emmy win for Outstanding Younger Actress, Allen, 25, says, "It feels amazing. And when I found out that Oscar winner Melissa Leo started on *All My Children*, that was great to learn."

CHRISTOPHER LAWFORD
CHARLIE BRENT
The new U.N. Goodwill Ambassador for drug-dependence treatment and care appreciated his stint on daytime TV. The Kennedy family scion and recovering addict, 56, remembers "the story we did about alcoholism and codependency. It meant something to people." He remembers other stories too: "I took Kelly Ripa's virginity, and that was a great honor!"

GILLIAN SPENCER

DAISY CORTLANDT
When her run on *AMC* ended in 1989, Spencer, now 71, joined the show's writing team. Later she moved south and expanded her horizons. "I'm what's called a medical intuitive," she says. "I work with physicians and people in the healing professions, working with patients who are having trouble finding treatments."

CAMERON MATHISON

RYAN LAVERY

"They didn't call me 'Snaps' on *All My Children* for nothing," the ex-Hugo Boss model—who has a track record for baring his chest on the soap—once joked. "All my shirts had snaps on them for easy removal!"

Decades of HOT GUYS

Some started out as models, some became heartthrobs after they hit Pine Valley, but all these men made one thing powerfully clear: *All My Children* sure knows how to turn up the heat on daytime TV

NICHOLAS BENEDICT
PHIL BRENT

AMC has a long history of supplying eye candy for its fans. Benedict, whose character had just returned from Vietnam, made his mark as one of the first.

COLIN EGGLESFIELD
JOSH MADDEN

In 2005 the former Versace model pulled off a rare one-two punch of hunkdom: nabbing his role on *AMC* (he played Erica's son) and landing on PEOPLE's Sexiest Man Alive list. These days Egglesfield, 38, is still acting; he popped up in the film *Something Borrowed* and on TV's *Hawaii Five-0* revamp.

AIDEN TURNER
AIDAN DEVANE

"I'd get the script two days before and gasp, 'I'm in my underpants? You could have given me five days notice!'" recalls the 34-year-old British actor (he's currently playing the role of a male model in the VH1 drama *Single Ladies*). "It's awkward. But you have to remember your lines and remember not to block camera two, so it's a lot to think about, and I'd just forget that I was half naked."

CORNELIUS SMITH JR.
FRANKIE HUBBARD

"I do lip push-ups to prepare for the kissing scenes," says Smith. "No, I'm just playing. But you definitely want to make sure your breath is good. So you pop some gum, ask if anybody has a mint, and you're ready to go."

DANIEL COSGROVE
SCOTT CHANDLER

Like many of his beefcake brethren, the 40-year-old Cosgrove has not been shy about appearing on *AMC* shirtless or even sporting nothing but a towel.

JACOB YOUNG

J.R. CHANDLER

"J.R. is caught between good and evil all the time," says Young. "And that makes him an extremely alluring character."

JUSTIN BRUENING
JAMIE MARTIN

Bruening—a former Abercrombie & Fitch model—recalls the moment he hooked up with his main onscreen love interest, Babe Chandler. "We met at a little beach party," says Bruening. "We kissed, and five hours later we were having sex. I was so charming that one scene later, we were having sex."

KEITH HAMILTON COBB
NOAH KEEFER

"It was my first major nontheater gig," says Cobb, now 49, of his 2½ year stint on *AMC*, during which the actor also made it onto PEOPLE's list of the 50 Most Beautiful People. Since leaving Pine Valley, the actor has done prime-time TV and more stage work, but Noah still resonates. "The character made quite an impact," says Cobb. "I was blessed to have a huge cross section of fans: Everyone from 8-year-olds watching with their moms to gay men to Jewish grandmothers gravitated to him."

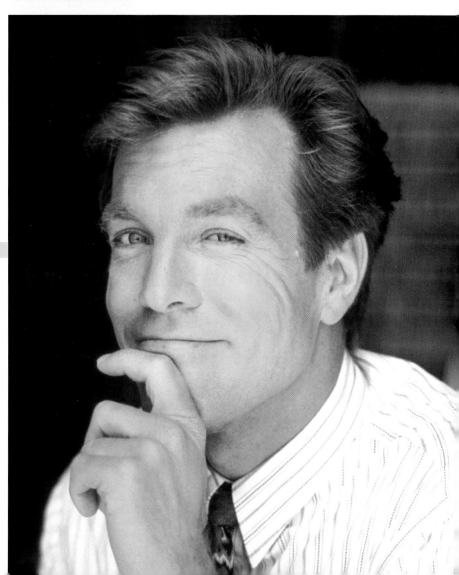

PETER BERGMAN
DR. CLIFF WARNER

Being a daytime soap hunk doesn't guarantee a major self-esteem boost. "I once rode a train out to Long Island to visit a friend, and a woman across the train looked at me and smiled," recalls *AMC* alumnus Bergman, 58, a married father of two and current *Young and the Restless* star. "I said to myself, 'Obviously, she watches the show. She recognizes me!' So as I got off the train, I gave her a knowing smile as if to say, 'Yes, I am who you think I am.' And she said, 'Are you a waiter at Rusty's?' The thing is, I had been a waiter at Rusty's. That's where she recognized me from."

JOSH DUHAMEL
LEO DU PRES

Transitioning from a modeling career (he beat out Ashton Kutcher for the title of Male Model of the Year in 1997), Duhamel struck gold on *All My Children*; he won an Emmy for his role as a seductive con artist. He also made it into PEOPLE's Sexiest Man Alive issue four times.

MICHAEL E. KNIGHT
TAD MARTIN

"When you're young and you do personal appearances and you throw kisses and make the fans scream, it's hard to take seriously," says Martin, flashing back to his early, hysteria-inducing *AMC* days. "But I gotta say I enjoyed the hell out of it."

RICHARD HATCH
PHIL BRENT

Hatch, now 66 and still acting, got his start on *AMC*, but later appeared on TV shows ranging from *Baywatch* to *Battlestar Galactica*.

MARK CONSUELOS
MATEO SANTO
Before he became an *AMC* heartthrob, Consuelos had to screen-test with his future wife, Kelly Ripa (Hayley). "I wasn't thinking about getting lucky," he told PEOPLE in 1999. "I was worried about getting the job."

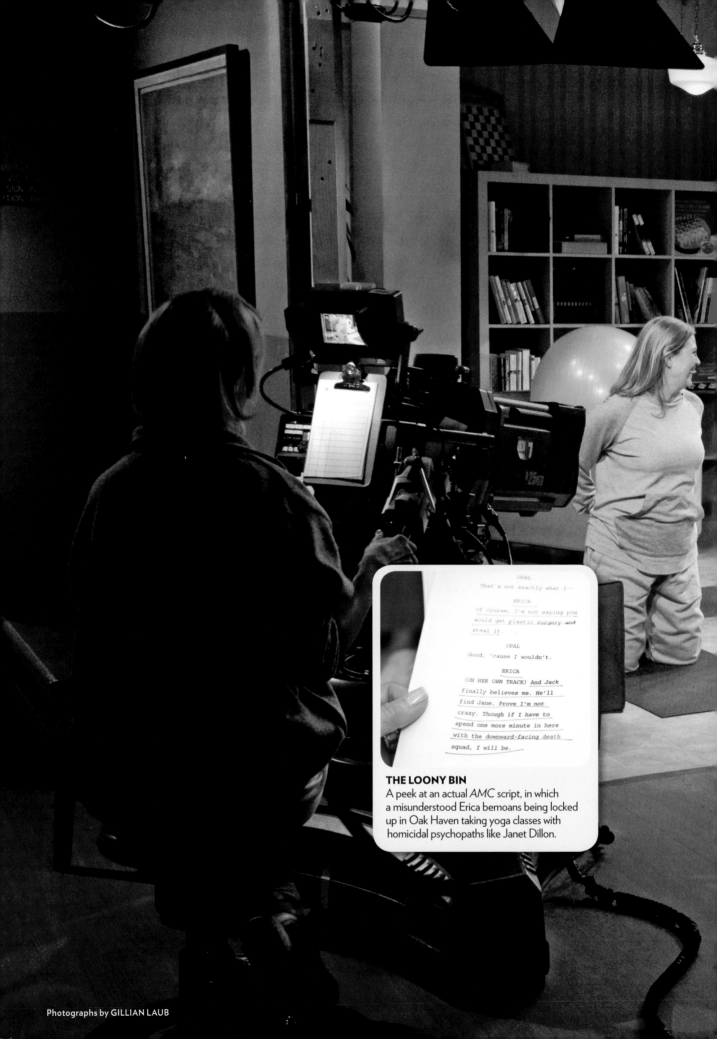

OPAL

That's not exactly what I--

ERICA

Of course, I'm not saying you would get plastic surgery and steal it...

OPAL

Good, 'cause I wouldn't.

ERICA

(ON HER OWN TRACK) And Jack finally believes me. He'll find Jane. Prove I'm not crazy. Though if I have to spend one more minute in here with the downward-facing death squad, I will be.

THE LOONY BIN
A peek at an actual *AMC* script, in which a misunderstood Erica bemoans being locked up in Oak Haven taking yoga classes with homicidal psychopaths like Janet Dillon.

BEHIND THE SCENES

Life on-set: A backstage peek at rehearsals, the makeup room and the practical jokes

Soundstage

The goings-on at Oak Haven, where Erica meets Pine Valley's favorite crazies from the past, have been created inside the L.A. studio complex where the show is filmed

The Makeup Room

The spot for last-minute beauty touch-ups is also
a popular place for costar gab sessions

A BAD SIGN

Although his castmates have their real names posted on their dressing-room doors, Vincent Irizarry gets a "Dr. Evil" sign. But Irizarry defends his villainous character Dr. David Hayward, saying simply, "He's complex!"

WORDS OF WISDOM

Somebody tacked up this Botox comment next to a cast list. Says Ricky Paull Goldin of the sense of humor that pervades the set: "I laugh the most in my life while I'm at work."

BLUSH AND BONDING

As Melissa Claire Egan (seated) gets prepped for a scene, she multitasks by catching up with costar Chrishell Stause (center). "Chrishell became one of my best friends right away," says Egan. "We're attached at the hip!"

KEEPING ALL THE STORIES STRAIGHT

For continuity's sake, all of the characters' accessories are neatly organized and labeled. That way Dr. Jake Martin is never without his name tag, and Ryan can avoid having to explain why his wedding band is missing.

CHARACTER BUILDING

"Everyone was patient with me," says J.R. Martinez, who got his on-the-job acting training on *AMC*. "I started to watch and grow. This has been my school of hard knocks."

SIGNATURE STYLE

"In the beginning they smoothed my hair out, but it didn't look good," says Alicia Minshew. "So I said, 'Can we just go with my natural curl and bump it up?' After that they said, 'Okay, this is Kendall's look. She's the chick with the curly hair.'"

COMMAND CENTER

In the control room in the Glendale, Calif., studio, crew members monitor various camera angles during filming. No surprise, at the moment captured here, Erica is center stage.

Dressing Room

The place where Susan Lucci relaxes between scenes

LEARNING HER LINES

Memorizing pages and pages of script every day has become second nature to Susan Lucci. "It's kind of like cramming for a chemistry exam," she says. "I read and reread, but when the script is well-written, you can just follow the train of thought. That's important."

Dressing
THE CAST

Each character has a color palette.
Clothes are built for lovemaking!
Some stars wear their own pieces.
Secrets from Emmy-winning costume
designer David Zyla

"My job is to make these characters who come into your living room every day pop off the screen and come alive!" says David Zyla, the Emmy-winning force behind the show's costumes. To do that, he gives his stars their own signature colors (Kendall's palette, for example, is amethyst and dove grey, while Erica wears black, fire engine red and parrot green) and he equips his team of shoppers with words to describe each character (Opal is "crisp,

A PLACE FOR EVERYTHING

Each character "requires thought as to who they are, because we want a believability," says costume designer David Zyla (far left) fitting actress Alicia Minshew (Kendall) in her signature color. Below, pieces are marked with characters' names and kept in a "trailer" adjacent to the studio.

erica earrings
only rhinestones

erica rings/brooches

erica earrings
silver setting
no rhinestones   2 of 3

erica sentimental
please tag each jewelry piece w/event or script

erica earrings
silver setting
no rhinestones   1 of 3

erica earrings
silver setting
no rhinestones   3 of 3

erica
gold setting
no rhinest   Unmatched
Earings

Small dangly rhinestone ea
Gold and silver setting

bead/stone pendants
not faceted

erica earrings
gold setting
no rhinestones   1 of 3

CHOO

052 KEEN   Dk Gold Laminated Nappa   36
Lamina

ERICA

ERICA

STUART
WEITZMAN

MARIANI
Studio

MODELING AT THE MET

"Those were some of my good days, because I'm never going to be a fashion model, but I love fashion," says Susan Lucci of Erica Kane's 1983 foray into modeling at the Metropolitan Museum of Art in N.Y.C.

theatrical, zany"; Angie is "natural, chic, feminine"). They scour stores and showrooms from as far away as Europe and South America for a look that's "not avant-garde, but just ahead of the curve," says Zyla. Like the rest of us, the denizens of Pine Valley wear their clothes repeatedly —"but I'm extremely clever about that" says Zyla. "If Opal wears a white suit, you might see that skirt again, but it will be accessorized differently. Because the story is going forward, I want the clothes to go forward." After Kendall had children, for instance, "she softened up a bit. She's still very sexy, but at a certain point we had to put clothes in her wardrobe that would be appropriate for holding a baby." Some plots call for Zyla to design the clothes himself. "People in Pine Valley are very amorous!" he says. "I love 'build-to-lovemaking' blouses that unbutton, unsnap or unwrap easily." Every once in a while, Zyla lets the stars contribute from their own wardrobes. "Recently Rebecca Budig, who plays Greenlee, had a personal watch we've incorporated. And so did Cameron Mathison." After eight years on the job (plus three more at other soaps), Zyla relates to the characters. "This is very different from doing a film," he says. "This is every day, and these characters grow. We're not just capturing a moment."

BAGS GALORE !
Accessories and clothes are rotated each season; "off-season" items are stored in a separate building.

MARDI GRAS BALL
Erica wears a dress by costume designer Zyla to a 2006 bash. "We did 17 women's gowns for that ball," says Zyla. "When there's a special occasion, we design the clothes ourselves."

Pine Valley Wedding Album

A toast to the some of the most elaborate nuptials in daytime TV history

NINA & CLIFF

TAYLOR MILLER AND PETER BERGMAN

The 1980 union of Cliff Warner and Nina Cortlandt was one
of *AMC*'s most highly anticipated and extravagantly produced
weddings. But the affair—which was shot over two days in
New Canaan, Conn.—turned out to be much more satisfying
for viewers than for the actors. "Peter wasn't feeling well, and it
didn't feel all that special," recalls Miller. "But when we saw what
they shot, it was amazing." Adds Bergman: "It was larger than
life—as big a shoot as daytime had seen. It was giant."

MARIA & EDMUND

**EVA LA RUE AND
JOHN CALLAHAN**

For the 1994 wedding of Maria
Santos and Edmund Grey, the cast
journeyed to a cathedral in New
Jersey. "We drove up in a horse-
drawn carriage," recalls La Rue of the
wintertime shoot. "Luckily, it was like
65° outside. It was gorgeous."

ERICA & DIMITRI
SUSAN LUCCI AND MICHAEL NADER

Of Erica Kane's many weddings, her 1993 ceremony with husband No. 7 ranks right up there with her favorites. "It was Russian Orthodox," says Lucci. "We did a traditional ceremony with lots and lots of candles. It was very beautiful."

OPAL & PALMER
JILL LARSON AND JAMES MITCHELL

At her 1990 wedding, Opal Purdy drew big laughs when she sped through her vows to get to her big kiss with Palmer Cortlandt. Their marriage was one of the longest-lasting on the show, ending two years before Palmer (and Mitchell) passed away in 2010.

JENNY & GREG
KIM DELANEY AND LAURENCE LAU

Jenny Gardner was serene when she wed her high school sweetheart Greg Nelson in 1984, but the same can't be said for the woman who played her. "I couldn't eat," Delaney told PEOPLE at the time. "It's like a real wedding!"

JULIA & NOAH
SYDNEY PENNY AND KEITH HAMILTON COBB

"My life didn't start until you," said Julia Santos as she wed Noah Keefer in 1996, delighting fans, who rooted for the couple even when their own onscreen relatives didn't. "After Noah died, they tried pairing Sydney with others, but nothing took off," says Hamilton Cobb of the couple's legacy. "In the viewers' minds, we were an entity."

JESSE & ANGIE
DARNELL WILLIAMS AND DEBBI MORGAN

To the delight of fans, Angie Baxter and a resurrected Jesse Hubbard remarried in 2008, as Ne-Yo crooned his song "Stop This World" in the background.

PHIL & TARA
RICHARD HATCH AND KAREN LYNN GORNEY

Tara Martin and Phillip Brent had a winding road to happiness, but they finally made it official in 1976. Recalls Gorney of the union: "It was quite spiritual."

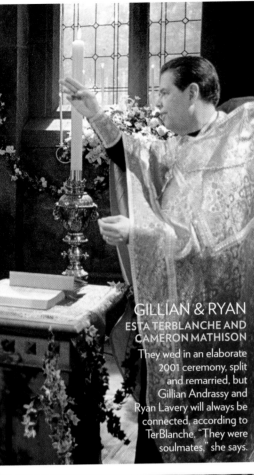

GILLIAN & RYAN
ESTA TERBLANCHE AND CAMERON MATHISON

They wed in an elaborate 2001 ceremony, split and remarried, but Gillian Andrassy and Ryan Lavery will always be connected, according to TerBlanche. "They were soulmates," she says.

DIXIE & TAD
CADY McCLAIN AND MICHAEL E. KNIGHT

"I should know this by now!" giggled Dixie Cooney as she pledged her undying love and affection to Tad Martin at their second wedding, in 1994. (They split and remarried, a third time too.) Says Knight: "Anyone who came in after Dixie was measured against her."

REESE & BIANCA
TAMARA BRAUN AND EDEN RIEGEL

In the show's only gay wedding, Bianca Montgomery wed Reese Williams, only to have it annulled the next day. Still, the 2009 union was historic. Says Riegel: "I stood up for the gay population."

WHAT'S INSIDE THE LIQUOR BOTTLES?

"They used to use colored water," says set decorator KayDee Lavorin. "Now it's mostly watered-down iced tea. The actors were pleasantly surprised because it tastes like something!"

WHY IS THERE STILL A PAY PHONE?

"This was a prop for a particular story point," says production designer Jim Jones. "Caleb [Michael Nouri] refused to have a cell phone, so we had to have a pay phone. It just stayed there."

Krystal's

The restaurant and bar where the food is bad but the gossip is good

SECRETS FROM THE SET

What's really on the menus, in the hospital records, among the photo displays and more

ARE THOSE REAL FLOWERS ONSTAGE?

"Yes, all of the close-up table flowers are fresh," reports Lavorin. "Our florist shows up every morning, and there they are!"

WHAT'S WRITTEN ON THE MENUS?

Actual food options! "I found menus from my favorite restaurants and pulled up what a good bistro menu offers," says Lavorin. "We also added accurate prices."

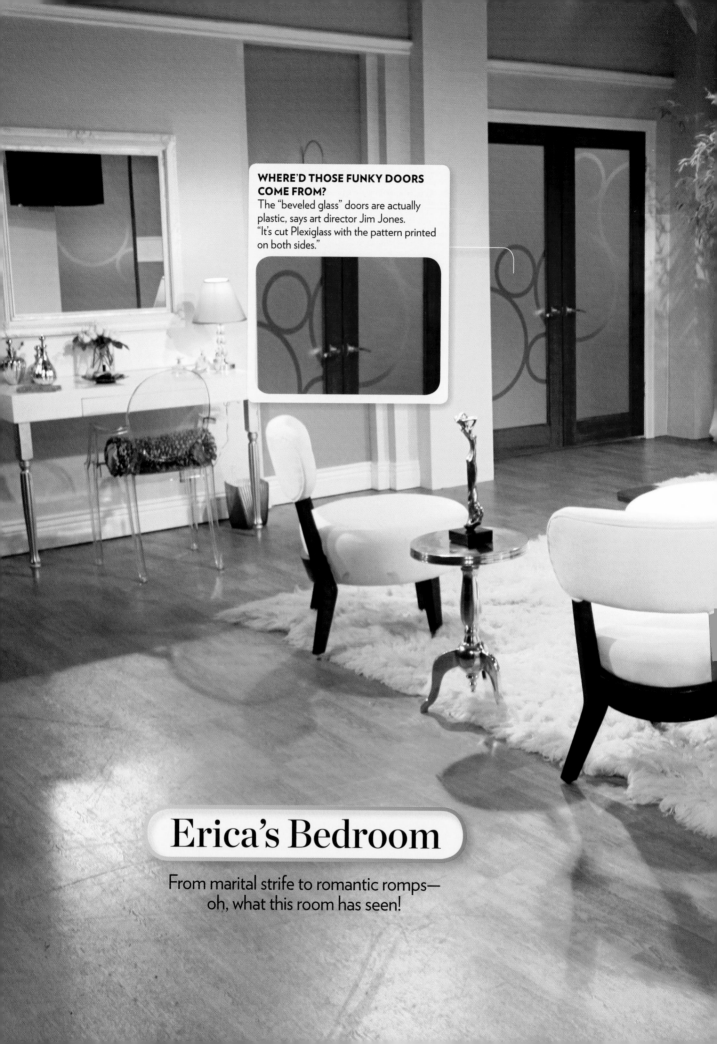

WHERE'D THOSE FUNKY DOORS COME FROM?
The "beveled glass" doors are actually plastic, says art director Jim Jones. "It's cut Plexiglass with the pattern printed on both sides."

Erica's Bedroom

From marital strife to romantic romps—
oh, what this room has seen!

HOW LUXE IS ERICA'S DECOR?
For the Pine Valley chic look, "we used Pottery Barn bedding and Z Gallerie furnishings," says set decorator KayDee Lavorin. "The throws I'll mix in from less expensive stores."

HOW OFTEN DOES THAT RUG GET SHAMPOOED?
Although it has seen its fair share of foot traffic, the truth is "we usually only clean on an as-needed basis," Jones admits.

DO THE MEGARICH CHANDLERS LIVE MORE REGALLY?
In fact they do. "I had a furniture-maker build these sofas," says set decorator KayDee Lavorin. "They also made the side tables and the ottomans."

WHERE DO THE PHOTOS COME FROM?
"We love to use personal photos when available," says Lavorin. "But the great thing about this show is that there's a big archive of photos through the years."

The Chandler Mansion

The home passed down through generations of scoundrels

WHO CREATES THE ART ON THE WALLS?
"You won't see any terribly famous pieces for copyright reasons," says production designer Jim Jones. "Eighty percent of our artwork is from a prop house or some kind of a gallery."

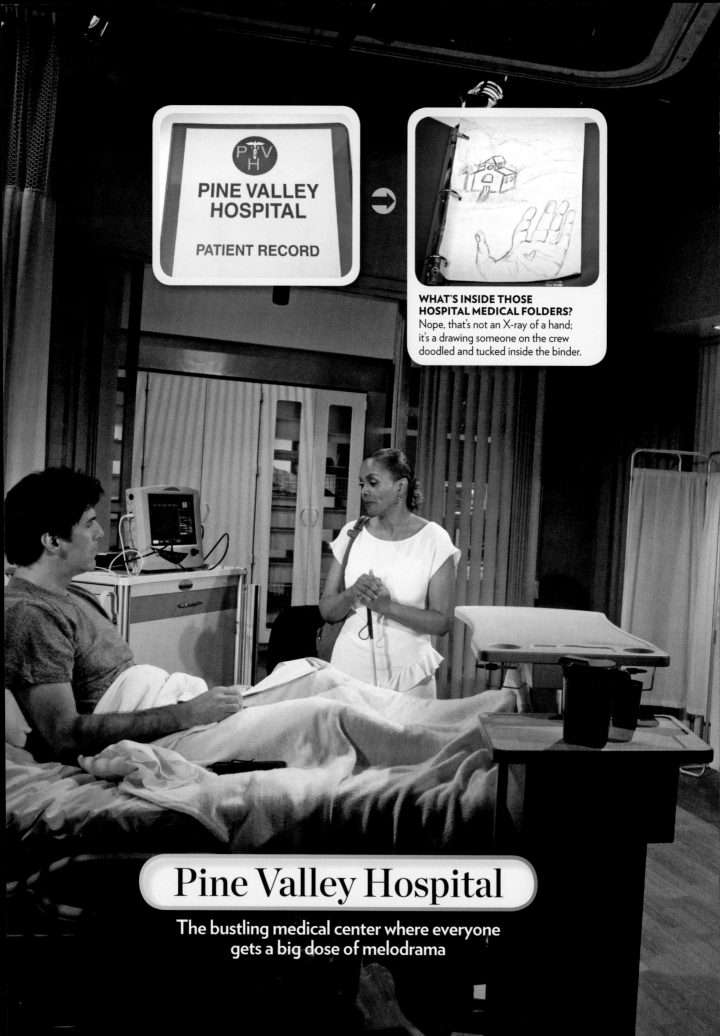

PINE VALLEY HOSPITAL

PATIENT RECORD

WHAT'S INSIDE THOSE HOSPITAL MEDICAL FOLDERS?
Nope, that's not an X-ray of a hand; it's a drawing someone on the crew doodled and tucked inside the binder.

Pine Valley Hospital

The bustling medical center where everyone gets a big dose of melodrama

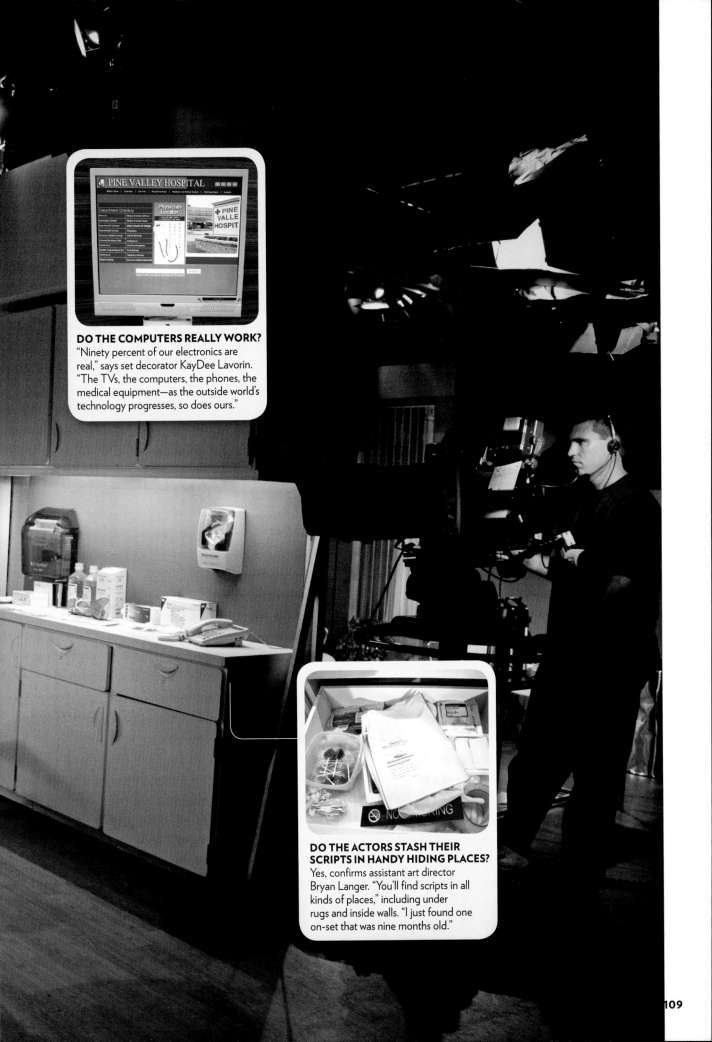

DO THE COMPUTERS REALLY WORK?
"Ninety percent of our electronics are real," says set decorator KayDee Lavorin. "The TVs, the computers, the phones, the medical equipment—as the outside world's technology progresses, so does ours."

DO THE ACTORS STASH THEIR SCRIPTS IN HANDY HIDING PLACES?
Yes, confirms assistant art director Bryan Langer. "You'll find scripts in all kinds of places," including under rugs and inside walls. "I just found one on-set that was nine months old."

JOSH DUHAMEL
LEO DU PRES

"The first time I was on-set, I couldn't breathe," recalls the actor, 38, who overcame the initial nerves and won a Daytime Emmy for his work on *AMC*. Even after going on to prime time and films, Duhamel couldn't resist returning to *AMC* at the end of its run. "They gave me my first opportunity," he says. "It was such a great launching pad—and a great job."

We Knew Them When...

Action heroes, teen idols, a talk show host—and an Oscar winner—who got their start on *All My Children*

MELISSA LEO
LINDA WARNER

She's the reigning Best Supporting Actress Oscar winner for her role in *The Fighter*, but Leo, 50, still looks back fondly on some of the scrapes she got into in Pine Valley as the troubled sister of Dr. Cliff Warner. "I loved that part," Leo has said. "When all is said and done, I can say that I was a part of the great American soap opera."

EVA LA RUE
DR. MARIA SANTOS GREY

La Rue's first year on the *AMC* set was the college experience she never had. "It felt like a big sorority," says the *CSI: Miami* star, 44, who has remained close with former costars Sarah Michelle Gellar and Kelly Ripa. "Kelly's husband, Mark, came on *AMC* as my character's brother, and the two of them fell in love at the same time that my ex John Callahan [another *AMC* star] and I were falling in love," she recalls. "It was a something-in-the-water kind of thing over there!" La Rue was thrilled when her wish was granted to return to Pine Valley before the show's finale. Says the actress: "I really wanted to be a part of the end."

LEVEN RAMBIN
**SISTERS
LILY MONTGOMERY
& AVA BENTON**

Rambin, 21, says getting to play both autistic Lily and prostitute Ava was "a gift." She's now filming *The Hunger Games* after a stint on *Grey's Anatomy,* but she's still close with old castmates including Ambyr Childers (Colby Chandler). "She's one of my best friends," says Rambin. "I'm her child's godmother!"

LAUREN HOLLY
JULIE CHANDLER

Holly, who had only acted in commercials before landing her *AMC* role, still remembers the thrill of filming her first scene. "I had two sentences to say, and I was so nervous, it took me three days to memorize them," says the actress, 47. But her fondest memories are of the actors who played her parents, Kathleen Noone (Ellen Dalton) and Robert Gentry (Ross Chandler). "Kathy was like a cup of tea—the warmest person," says Holly. "And Bob, who was into woodworking, made me the greatest big table from an old barn. It's the one in my family room that everyone puts their feet up and plays board games on."

AMANDA SEYFRIED
JONI STAFFORD

Her 10-month gig on *AMC* holds a storied place in the 25-year-old *Red Riding Hood* star's life. "I got cast in *All My Children,* where I met my first love, who introduced me to my manager. He was the reason I got *Mean Girls,*" Seyfried—who played an ultra-religious high schooler on the soap—told *Backstage* in 2010. That sure beats her stint on *As the World Turns.* "I was so bad they had to ship my character off!" said Seyfried.

KELLY RIPA
HAYLEY VAUGHAN SANTOS

She has cohosted *Live with Regis & Kelly* since 2001, but Ripa hasn't changed much since her days playing Adam Chandler's daughter. "I watch her morning show, and she has the exact same personality she had back then," recalls Ripa's former castmate Lacey Chabert. "Very approachable, funny and kind." Adds Ripa's onscreen brother Jesse McCartney: "She was always good for laughs. When the spaghetti straps on her tops would break, she would yell at wardrobe, 'That's what happens when you use dental floss to hold these things together!'" Ripa was nominated for three Daytime Emmys for her work on the show. "It was a great life, and I wouldn't have traded it for anything," she has said.

LACEY CHABERT
BIANCA MONTGOMERY

Chabert was the third actress to play Bianca when she took over the role at 9 years old. "It helped prepare me for my years on *Party of Five*. It created a great work ethic," says the actress, 28, who went on to star in *Mean Girls* and *Lost in Space*. "As a kid, I was in *Les Misérables* on Broadway eight times a week, and then I got to play Susan Lucci's daughter! When you're young, you don't take all of that in. But looking back on that journey, I'm so grateful."

JESSE McCARTNEY
ADAM CHANDLER JR.

"My first month on the show, both my sister Hayley [Kelly Ripa] and I got kidnapped," recalls the pop star and actor, 24, who was twice nominated for a Daytime Emmy. "I still have the photo of us from that episode in my house—we were locked in a cage!"

SARAH MICHELLE GELLAR
KENDALL HART

Before she starred in *Buffy the Vampire Slayer*, Gellar, 34, originated the role of Erica Kane's daughter Kendall Hart, winning a Daytime Emmy for her portrayal of one of the most devious daughters on television. "The key is to have fun being evil," she has said. "When you enjoy it, the audience enjoys it."

KIM DELANEY
JENNY GARDNER NELSON

Delaney, 49, who now stars on *Army Wives*, has a favorite memory from her time on the show. "[Guest star] Carol Burnett took me and some castmates out to a fancy dinner and told us to appreciate what we had because it doesn't always happen this way. We took her advice and savored every moment."

COLIN EGGLESFIELD
JOSH MADDEN

Looking back, the actor, 38, relished his character's twisted story lines, from his beginnings as the transplanted fetus of Erica Kane to his untimely end as a heart donor for half-sister Kendall Hart. "Sometimes it's frustrating; sometimes it's pretty funny," he's said of being on *AMC*, "but the great thing about it is it always keeps you on your toes."

LINDSAY PRICE
AN-LI CHEN BODINE

When Price, 34, started on *All My Children* as a teenager, she became fast friends with another young actress trying to make it in New York—Sarah Michelle Gellar, who joined the cast about a year and a half later. "It was neat because Sarah became my closest friend. We hit it off," Price has said. In fact the friends were so close that they even shared a dressing room.

ROSIE O'DONNELL, 1996

The same summer that she launched her eponymous TV talk show, O'Donnell appeared in an episode as Adam Chandler's hilariously unprofessional maid Naomi.

Celeb CAMEOS

There are a lot of perks to being famous, but for these stars, one of the biggest was getting the chance to be on their favorite soap

THE NEW ORLEANS SAINTS, 1981
"The show was huge with sports teams who watched while having lunch during practices," says executive producer Julie Hanan Carruthers. The *AMC*-loving Saints made an appearance helping Erica shoot a commercial for her cosmetics line in the Louisiana Superdome.

THE OLSEN TWINS, 1998
A few years after *Full House* ended, 12-year-old Mary-Kate and Ashley made cameos as themselves on *AMC*.

RICHARD SIMMONS, 1995
The fitness guru had Erica sweating to the oldies during an appearance on her talk show.

RIHANNA, 2006
At the opening of Pine Valley's hottest new club—ConFusion—the singer gave a special performance of her single "S.O.S."

STEVIE WONDER, 1986
The Grammy winner sang a duet of "I Just Called to Say I Love You" with Erica and then crooned two songs on his own.

[C]ELINE DION, 2007
[Th]e singer, appearing as herself,
[sto]pped by to chat with Erica
[dur]ing an episode of the Pine
[Vall]ey diva's talk show.

MONTEL WILLIAMS, 2002
The talk show host played
the presiding judge when
Erica Kane was being tried
for murder.

MEREDITH VIEIRA, 2001
A fan of the show since high
school, Vieira played the
dotty wedding planner in
charge of the big day for
Leo (Josh Duhamel) and
Laura (Laura Allen).

DOM DeLUISE, 1991
The funnyman played a cop who helped reunite a young Hayley (Kelly Ripa) with her beloved uncle Trevor (James Kiberd).

ELIZABETH TAYLOR, 1983 & 1984
She first appeared as a board member of Pine Valley's Chateau restaurant and later (above, with Carol Burnett) popped up as a scrubwoman at the Goal Post.

"Why I love *All My Children*"

—by Carol Burnett

My daughters actually got me into the show. It was a summer vacation, and they would come home for lunch and run right to the television to watch *All My Children*. I started watching it with them, and I got hooked. Jeff was married to Mary. That's how long ago it was.

One summer, my husband and I went to Europe, and I had a friend of mine send me a telegram every Friday to bring me up to date on what was going on in Pine Valley. I remember one day we checked into the hotel in Lake Como, and around 2:00 in the morning there was a knock on the door and the manager of the hotel was just standing there shaking, his face as pale as could be. He gave me a telegram. It said, "Erica's still missing. Phoebe has amnesia and Mona is going on trial for murder." I started laughing hysterically and he thought I was crying and went to get me a Valium to calm me down. Then my husband said, "Oh for God's sake, it's her soap." So much bad news in one message!

When Agnes Nixon came up with the character of Verla Grubbs, I adored her. I got to talk Southern and be a little trashy. It was fun. And everyone really welcomed me into the fold. Now I've been a fan for well over 30 years, and it's been great fun to watch. It's gonna leave a little gap in my life. They will be sorely missed.

CAROL BURNETT, 1983
The comedian appeared as Verla Grubbs, the long-lost daughter of Langley Wallingford (Louis Edmonds).

In Memoriam

Tributes to the late stars of *All My Children*

RUTH WARRICK
1916-2005
(Phoebe Tyler Wallingford)

She made her screen debut opposite Orson Welles in *Citizen Kane*, costarred with Debbie Reynolds on Broadway and counted Gene Kelly and Bob Hope as close friends, but her *AMC* costars attest that Warrick was just as young at heart as she was Old Hollywood. "Ruthie was wild!" recalls Linda Gibboney (Sybil Thorne). "She would flash the cameramen, meet guys and ask me to double-date with her. We'd go dancing and have cocktails. She was fun." Of course, she also loved her glamour. "Ruth heard I was going to Club Med one time and wanted to come," says Jennifer Bassey (Marian Colby). "She arrived with two trunks filled with feather boas, diamonds and evening gowns—she was Gloria Swanson in *Sunset Boulevard*."

In Memoriam

EILEEN HERLIE
1918-2008
(Myrtle Fargate)

She always told the best stories," remembers Michael E. Knight of *AMC*'s affable innkeeper. "I loved to hear her talk about her youth in Hollywood." Herlie's big-break screen role was playing the mother of Hamlet (portrayed by Laurence Olivier) in the 1948 film. She also earned a Tony nomination for her work in the 1960 musical *Take Me Along*, and during her *AMC* stint she nabbed three Emmy nominations. Says Knight: "She was something else."

LOUIS EDMONDS
1923-2001
(Langley Wallingford)

He first burst onto the soap-opera scene in the '60s-era gothic sensation *Dark Shadows*, but Edmonds made his most lasting impression as *AMC*'s ever-imperial Langley, for which he earned three Emmy nominations. "He was a creative spirit who approached his work as an art," says costar Mark La Mura (Mark Dalton). "He was a real card. A wonderful, wonderful man."

LYNNE THIGPEN
1948-2003
(Grace Keefer)

PAUL GLEASON
1939-2006
(Dr. David Thornton)

DACK RAMBO
1941-1994
(Steve Jacobi)

KAY CAMPBELL
1904-1985
(Kate Martin No. 3)

KATE HARRINGTON
1902-1978
(Kate Martin No. 1)

LARRY KEITH
1931–2010
(Nick Davis)

ELIZABETH LAWRENCE
1922–2000
(Myra Murdock)

NANCY ADDISON
1946–2002
(Marissa Rampal)

RAUL DAVILA
1931–2006
(Hector Santos)

JAMES MITCHELL
1920–2010
(Palmer Cortlandt)

Mitchell was one of the patriarchs of Pine Valley, as well as a father figure to his costars. "When we first started working together, he kind of adopted me," says Taylor Miller, who played his daughter Nina. "He was so dear to me, plus he was hysterical, he made Palmer such a funny bad guy." Gillian Spencer, who starred as his wife, Daisy, also gushes about Mitchell's work ethic. "Every gesture we made together was carefully timed out because he was so detailed, like a dancer," she recalls. "He was just a lovely, lovely being."

FRANCES HEFLIN
1920–1994
(Mona Kane Tyler)

The theater veteran acted opposite Susan Lucci during their screen tests in 1970, and the two hit it off. "She was very sophisticated and very bright," says Lucci, who played her daughter. "She did the *New York Times* crossword puzzle in ink!" Even now, the loss of Heflin leaves Lucci a bit misty. "She was very affirming for me, and I admired her very much," she says. "To this day, I drive past her apartment, where I stayed many times, and I miss her."

HUGH FRANKLIN
1916–1986
(Dr. Charles Tyler)

Masthead

Editors Jamie Bufalino, Cynthia Sanz, Elizabeth Sporkin
Design Director Andrea Dunham **Director of Photography** Chris Dougherty
Editor-at-Large Antoinette Y. Coulton
Art Director Cynthia Rhett **Designers** Joan Dorney, Amy Jaffe, Daniel J. Neuburger
Art Production Director Georgine Panko **Photo Editor** Karen O'Donnell **Assistant Photo Editor** C. Tiffany Lee Ramos **Senior Writer** Lesley Messer **Writers** Liza Hamm,
Marisa Laudadio, Daniel S. Levy, Cynthia Wang **Correspondents** Michael Maloney,
Jenisha Watts **Reporters** Mary Hart, Paul Chi, Sabrina Ford, Jazmyn Tuberville,
Jennifer Wren **Copy** Joanann Scali (Copy Chief), James Bradley (Deputy),
Aura Davies (Copy Coordinator), Ellen Adamson, Jennifer Broughel,
Pearl Chen, Gabrielle Danchick, Valerie Georgoulakos, Lance Kaplan,
Alan Levine, Jennifer Shotz (Copy Editors) **Scanners** Brien Foy, Stephen Pabarue
Imaging Francis Fitzgerald (Imaging Director), Robert Roszkowski (Imaging
Manager), Romeo Cifelli, Charles Guardino (Imaging Coordinator Managers),
Jeffrey Ingledue **Administration** Patricia Hustoo-Reinhart
Special thanks to Céline Wojtala (Director), David Barbee, Jane Bealer,
Patricia Clark, Margery Frohlinger, Suzy Im, Ean Sheehy, Patrick Yang

TIME HOME ENTERTAINMENT

Publisher Richard Fraiman **Vice President, Business Development & Strategy**
Steven Sandonato **Executive Director, Marketing Services** Carol Pittard **Executive
Director, Retail & Special Sales** Tom Mifsud **Executive Director, New Product Development**
Peter Harper **Editorial Director** Steve Koepp **Director, Bookazine Development &
Marketing** Laura Adam **Publishing Director** Joy Butts **Finance Director** Glenn
Buonocore **Associate Director, Marketing and Communications** Malati Chavali
Assistant General Counsel Helen Wan **Book Production Manager** Suzanne Janso
Design & Prepress Manager Anne-Michelle Gallero **Brand Manager** Michela Wilde
Associate Brand Manager Melissa Joy Kong **Special thanks to** Christine Austin, Jeremy
Biloon, Jim Childs, Susan Chodakiewicz, Rose Cirrincione, Jacqueline Fitzgerald,
Carrie Hertan, Christine Font, Lauren Hall, Malena Jones, Mona Li, Robert
Marasco, Kimberly Marshall, Amy Migliaccio, Nina Mistry, Dave Rozzelle, Ilene
Schreider, Adriana Tierno, Alex Voznesenskiy, Jonathan White, Vanessa Wu

Credits

FRONT COVER
Photograph by Andrew Southam; Hair: Valerie Jackson; Makeup: 'TC' Thecla Luisi; Stylist: David Zyla; Black Dress: Ali Rahimi for Mon Atelier; Earrings and Ring: Michael M.; Insets (clockwise from top left) Steve Fenn/ABC Photo Archives/Getty Images; Deborah Feingold/Corbis; Ann Limongello/ABC Photo Archives

CONTENTS
(Clockwise from top left) Ann Limongello/ABC Photo Archives/Getty Images; Peter Yang; Greg Weiner; Gillian Laub; Peter Yang; Ann Limongello/ABC Photo Archives; ABC Photo Archives/Getty Images **4** Steve Fenn/ABC Photo Archives; **5** Steve Fenn/ABC Photo Archives/Getty Images

THE WOMAN BEHIND ERICA
7 Photographs by Andrew Southam; Hair: Valerie Jackson; Makeup: 'TC' Thecla Luisi; Stylist: David Zyla; Black Dress: Ali Rahimi for Mon Atelier; Earrings and Ring: Michael M; (Inside) Orange Dress: Catherine Deane; Bracelet: Soixante Neuf **8** Courtesy Susan Lucci; **10-11** (1st row, from left) ABC Photo Archives; ABC Photo Archives/Getty Images(5); Ann Limongello/ABC Photo Archives; ABC Photo Archives/Getty Images(2); ABC Photo Archives; (2nd row, from left) Steve Fenn/ABC Photo Archives; ABC Photo Archives/Getty Images; ABC Photo Archives; ABC Photo Archives/Getty Images; ABC Photo Archives; Ann Limongello/ABC Photo Archives; ABC Photo Archives/Getty Images; Ann Limongello/ABC Photo Archives; Douglas Dubler/ABC Photo Archives; ABC Photo Archives; (3rd row, from left) Ann Limongello/ABC Photo Archives/Getty Images(2); Douglas Dubler/ABC Photo Archives; Ann Limongello/ABC Photo Archives; ABC Photo Archives/Getty Images; Steve Fenn/ABC Photo Archives/Getty Images; Ann Limongello/ABC Photo Archives; Robert Milazzo/ABC Photo Archives; Ann Limongello/ABC Photo Archives; Virginia Sherwood/ABC Photo Archives; (4th row, from left) Ann Limongello/ABC Photo Archives/Getty Images; Virginia Sherwood/ABC Photo Archives; Steve Fenn/ABC Photo Archives/Getty Images; Jeff Neira/ABC Photo Archives; Heidi Gutman/ABC Photo Archives; Steve Fenn/ABC Photo Archives/Getty Images; Lou Rocco/ABC Photo Archives/Getty Images; Carol Kaelson/ABC Photo Archives/Getty Images; **12** Seth Poppel Yearbook Archive; **13** (clockwise from top left) Courtesy Susan Lucci; Benjamin Luzon/AP; Nancy Kaszerman/Zuma/Corbis; Chris Farina/Corbis **14** © 2011 Harpo, Inc. George Burns; **15** (top, from left) ABC Photo Archives/Getty Images; ABC Photo Archives; Steve Fenn/ABC Photo Archives; ABC Photo Archives; ABC Photo Archives/Getty Images; Ann Limongello/ABC Photo Archives/Getty Images(2); Virginia Sherwood/ABC Phtoto Archives/Getty Images; **16-17** Andrew Southam

The 1970s
18 Steve Fenn/ABC Photo Archives/Getty Images; **20-21** (clockwise from top left) ABC Photo Archives/Getty Images(2); ABC Photo Archives; ABC Photo Archives/Getty Images; Steve Fenn/ABC Photo Archives/Getty Images(2); Steve Fenn/ABC Photo Archives; Ann Limongello/ABC Photo Archives(2); ABC Photo Archives; **22-23** (clockwise from top left) ABC Photo Archives/Getty Images; Ann Limongello/ABC Photo Archives/Getty Images; Cathy Blavias/ABC Photo Archives/Getty Images; Robin Platzer/Twin Images

The 1980s
24 Ann Limongello/ABC Photo Archives/Getty Images; **26-27** (clockwise from top left) Steve Fenn/ABC Photo Archives; ABC Photo Archives; Donna Svennevik/ABC Photo Archives; ABC Photo Archives/Getty Images; ABC Photo Archives; Peter Yang; Cathy Blaivas/ABC Photo Archives/Getty Images; Ann Limongello/ABC Photo Archives; ABC Photo Archives/Getty Images; Armin Weigel/Getty Images; Ann Limongello/ABC Photo Archives/Getty Images; ABC Photo Archives; ABC Photo Archives/Getty Images; **28-29** ABC Photo Archives/Getty Images (5) **30** (clockwise from top left) ABC Photo Archives/Getty Images; Ann Limongello/ABC Photo Archives/Getty Images(2); **31** Donna Svennevik/ABC Photo Archives; Peter Yang

The 1990s
32 ABC Photo Archives; **34-35** (clockwise from top left) ABC Photo Archives/Getty Images; Cathy Blaivas/ABC Photo Archives/Getty Images; Ann Limongello/ABC Photo Archives; Lorenzo Bevilaqua/ABC Photo Archives; Jim Antonucci/ABC Photo Archives; Ann Limongello/ABC Photo Archives/Getty Images; Vince Bucci/AFP/Getty Images; Ann Limongello/ABC Photo Archives; Ann Limongello/ABC Photo Archives/Getty Images(2); Ann Limongello/ABC Photo Archives; **36-37** (clockwise from bottom left) ABC Photo Archives/Getty Images; Ann Limongello/ABC Photo Archives(2); Everett Collection; Ann Limongello/ABC Photo Archives/Getty Images (2); **38** Deborah Feingold/Corbis; **39** (clockwise from top left) Donna Svennevik/ABC Photo Archives/Getty Images; Donna Svennevik/ABC Photo Archives; E.J. Carr/ABC Photo Archives

The 2000s
40 Virginia Sherwood/ABC Photo Archives/Getty Images; **42-43** (clockwise from top left) Virginia Sherwood/ABC Photo Archives; Virginia Sherwood/ABC Photo Archives/Getty Images; Virginia Sherwood/ABC Photo Archives; Jeff Neira/ABC Photo Archives; Lou Rocco/ABC Photo Archives/AP; Anthony Randell/ABC Photo Archives; Donna Svennevik/ABC Photo Archives; Jeff Neira/ABC Photo Archives; Donna Svennevik/ABC Photo Archives; Virginia Sherwood/ABC Photo Archives; **44-45** (from left) Bob D'Amico/ABC; Chris Chavira/ABC/Getty Images(2); Craig Sjodin/ABC/Getty Images(2); **46** (clockwise from top left) Steve Fenn/ABC Photo Archives/Getty Images; Heidi Gutman/ABC Photo Archives; Rick Rowell/ABC Photo Archives/Getty Images; **47** Peter Yang

PHOTOBOOTH
48-65 Photographs by Peter Yang; Hair: Valerie Jackson, Asha Williams, Ellis Von Hampton; Makeup: 'TC' Thecla, Earl Nicholson, Terri Carter, Ellis Von Hampton, David Michaud; Stylist: David Zyla; **60** (from left) Ann Limongello/ABC Photo Archives(3); Ann Limongello/ABC Photo Archives/Getty Images; ABC Photo Archives; Lorenzo Bevilaqua/ABC Photo Archives/Getty Images

WHERE ARE THEY NOW
67 Ann Limongello/ABC Photo Archives/Getty Images; **68** (clockwise from top left) Virginia Sherwood/ABC Photo Archives/Getty Images; ABC Photo Archives/Getty Images; Heidi Gutman/ABC Photo Archives/Getty Images; ABC Photo Archives/Getty Images; Steve Fenn/ABC Photo Archives/Getty Images; Donna Svennevik/ABC Photo Archives/Getty Images; **69** (clockwise from top right) Roxy Rifken/Shooting Star; ABC Photo Archives/Getty Images; Ann Limongello/ABC Photo Archives/Getty Images; **70** (clockwise from top left) Owen Franken/ABC Photo Archives; Christopher Little/ABC Photo Archives; Jeff Neira/ABC Photo Archives/Getty Images; Donna Svennevik/ABC Photo Archives; ABC Photo Archives/Getty Images; **71** (clockwise from top left) Heidi Gutman/ABC Photo Archives; ABC Photo Archives; ABC Photo Archives(2); Courtesy Lamman Rucker; **72** Ann Limongello/ABC Photo Archives; **73** (clockwise from top left) Bill Morris/ABC Photo Archives; Donna Svennevik/ABC Photo Archives; Yolanda Perez/ABC Photo Archives; ABC Photo Archives; ABC Photo Archives/Getty Images; **74** (clockwise from top left) ABC Photo Archives(2); Robert Milazzo; Rick Rowell/ABC Photo Archives/Getty Images; ABC Photo Archives; Steve Fenn/ABC Photo Archives

DECADES OF HOT GUYS
76 Robert Milazzo; **78** (from top) ABC Photo Archives; John Paschal/JPI Studios; **79** (clockwise from left) Craig Sjodin/ABC Photo Archives/Getty Images; Jon McKee/Retna; Patrick Wymore/ABC Photo; **80** Isabel Snyder/Corbis Outline; **81** (clockwise from top left) Robert Milazzo; Michael Tammaro/Retna; Jon McKee/Shooting Star; **82** (clockwise from top) David Stoltz/Shooting Star; Ken Probst/Corbis; Yoram Kahana/Shooting Star; **83** Greg Weiner

BEHIND THE SCENES
84-89 Photographs by Gillian Laub

WARDROBE DEPARTMENT
90-91 Gillian Laub; **92** Bob Sacha/Getty Images; **93** (clockwise from top) Courtesy David Zyla/ABC; Donna Svennevik/ABC Photo Archives; Gillian Laub

A PINE VALLEY WEDDING ALBUM
94 Steve Fenn/ABC Photo Archives/Getty Images; **96** Steve Fenn/ABC Photo Archives/Getty Images; (inset) Steve Fenn/ABC Photo Archives/Getty Images; **97** Kimberly Butler/ABC Photo Archives; (inset) Ann Limongello/ABC Photo Archives; **98** (clockwise from bottom left) Ann Limongello/ABC Photo Archives(2); Bob Sacha/ABC Photo Archives/Getty Images; **99** Ann Limongello/ABC Photo Archives/Getty Images; (inset) Ann Limongello/ABC Photo Archives; **100-101** (clockwise from top left) Steve Fenn/ABC Photo Archives(2); Ann Limongello/ABC Photo Archives; Lou Rocco/ABC Photo Archives; ABC Photo Archives

SECRETS FROM THE SET
102-109 Photographs by Gillian Laub
104-105 Courtesy ABC

WE KNEW THEM WHEN
110 Virginia Sherwood/ABC Photo Archives/Getty Images; **112-113** (clockwise from top right) Ann Limongello/ABC Photo Archives/Getty Images; Ann Limongello/ABC Photo Archives; Jennifer Gonzales/ABC Photo Archives; Virginia Sherwood/ABC Photo Archives/Getty Images; Ann Limongello/ABC Photo Archives; Ann Limongello/ABC Photo Archives/Getty Images; **114** (clockwise from top left) ABC Photo Archives/Getty Images; Virginia Sherwood/ABC Photo Archives/Getty Images; Ann Limongello/ABC Photo Archives/Getty Images; Heidi Gutman/ABC Photo Archives; **115** (from left) Lorenzo Bevilaqua/ABC/Getty Images; Ann Limongello/ABC Photo Archives/Getty Images

CELEB CAMEOS
116 ABC Photo Archives; **117** ABC Photo Archives; **118** (clockwise from top left) ABC Photo Archives/Getty Images; Ann Limongello/ABC Photo Archives(2); Jeff Neira/ABC Photo Archives/Getty Images; **119** (clockwise from top) Lou Rocco/ABC Photo Archives/Getty Images; Lorenzo Bevilaqua/ABC Photo Archives; Donna Svennevik/ABC Photo Archives; **120-121** (clockwise from top left) Ann Limongello/ABC Photo Archives; Donna Svennevik/ABC Photo Archives; ABC Photo Archives

IN MEMORIUM
123 Ann Limongello/ABC Photo Archives; **124** (clockwise from bottom left) ABC Photo Archives/Getty Images; Ann Limongello/ABC Photo Archives; Ann Limongello/ABC Photo Archives/Getty Images; ABC Photo Archives/Getty Images(4); **125** ABC Photo Archives; Ann Limongello/ABC Photo Archives; ABC Photo Archives/Getty Images; Ann Limongello/ABC Photo Archives(2); Robert Milazzo/ABC Photo Archives

CREDITS
Scott Humbert/ABC Photo Archives

LAST PAGE
Photograph by Andrew Southam

BACK COVER
(Clockwise from top left) Ann Limongello/ABC Photo Archives/Getty Images(3); Steve Fenn/ABC Photo Archives; Donna Svennevik/ABC Photo Archives/Getty Images; Cathy Blaivas/ABC Photo Archives/Getty Images; Ann Limongello/ABC Photo Archives/Getty Images